IMAGES
of England

AROUND
PRESTON
THE SECOND SELECTION

The summer-house in Moor Park, Serpentine, seen here, probably, in spring 1896. This unusual summer-house, built in an African style, must have been a very pleasant spot on a sunny afternoon. Between the pillars can be seen the Northern slope of the park and the path which ran over to St Paul's Road and led, eventually, to the far reaches of the ancient moor, south of English Martyrs' church. The Serpentine area was developed in 1833, and was described by Anthony Hewitson as 'very sylvan and pleasing'. The man sitting by the summerhouse is John Garlington (1871-1955), the author's great-grandfather.

IMAGES
of England

AROUND
PRESTON
THE SECOND SELECTION

Compiled by
John Garlington

TEMPUS

Tempus Publishing Limited
The Mill, Brimscombe Port,
Stroud, Gloucestershire, GL5 2QG

ISBN 0 7524 2086 0

Typesetting and origination by
Tempus Publishing Limited
Printed in Great Britain by
Midway Clark Printing, Wiltshire

For Nina, Ruth and Beth

The opening of the bandstand in Avenham Park, summer 1903. Formal summer wear was *de rigueur* for this festive occasion, with not a bare arm, or head, in sight. The bandstand was the finishing touch to the park which had once been pasture known as Broad Field before 1863. Children's festivals, or pageants, took place here from 1922 but up to then the park had been used for brass band concerts, fireworks displays and balloon ascents. The lime trees on Riverside, planted in 1863, stand out against an industrial summer haze, probably not uncommon at this time. This bandstand, which cost £450 to build, was taken down in 1952 and replaced by a larger one nearer Riverside.

Contents

Tram No. 22 outside the Red Lion Hotel, Church Street, 1930. Built originally at English Electric in Preston in 1919, this tram had been bought with two others from Lincoln in 1929 to replace older stock being used for parts. The important point about these three trams is that they were of a low height design that made them suitable for the Ashton route which ran under Fylde Road Bridge. The Red Lion Hotel, now known as the Coach House, was once one of Preston's coaching inns. The first stage coach ran from the town in 1771 and by 1823 seventy-two left the town every Wednesday and by 1830, eighty-one. The arrival of canal traffic cut the number to only twelve in 1837. The last horse-drawn coach left Preston in 1842. By 1930 a private motor garage was operating in the old stables.

Introduction

In April 1999, while in York on a family holiday, I noticed in a Waterstone's bookshop a copy of *York: The Second Selection*, by Amanda Howard in the Archive Photograph Series. I was very familiar with Amanda's first York book, but on seeing the newer one I began thinking about the possibilities of a second Preston selection. Encouragement from family and friends, factors at work and a telephone conversation with David Buxton of Tempus made me decide to go ahead.

When I began preparations, even before I drafted the first plans, I decided that the second selection, while acting as a complement to the first one, should stand in its own right as a book on Preston. Working on this principle, the first chapter, 'Uptown', looks in some depth at the medieval streets of the town, as in the first selection, but with entirely different pictures and commentaries. Choosing new chapter titles was sometimes a problem, but 'Uptown' came immediately and struck me as unusual. While people in neighbouring Lancashire towns often say 'downtown', Prestonians colloquially refer to their town centre as the opposite.

For the other chapters I followed the same principle. In 'Out of Town' I looked at the Victorian suburbs again, with a quick visit to Fulwood, but a longer look at Ashton, which had not been featured much before. 'Making Our Way' continues a look at the world of work in the town's commerce and industry. 'Beyond Our Sight' shows places and situations now literally out of sight. Some of these are ordinary and would have not caused much comment at the time but will be interesting to many now that they are gone.

While sorting through pictures and photographs some subjects begged to be covered. One of these was 'Making An Inroad' which traces the path of the new Arterial Road - Blackpool Road - in its infancy in the 1920s. Trams had been covered in the first selection so in 'Ways And Means' I took a more extended look at Preston's transport, bringing in buses and trains. There is one caveat, however; transport history is a complicated and technical subject, so here I confine myself to a limited but interesting selection.

To create a balance with the seriousness of some of the earlier chapters, the final pair, 'Along The River' and 'A Walk In The Park' should create an air of calm and well-being, with views of the Ribble from Redscar to Penwortham, and Avenham and Miller Parks.

At around the time I was writing the last few commentaries I picked up A.J. Berry's *Story of Preston* (1910) again. I have known this book since junior school at English Martyrs nearly forty years ago. I particularly noticed three items. The first was the remark that Preston 'has allowed many things that were hallowed by time to slip away, without making any effort to save them.' Prestonians know this to be true. Distinctive buildings have disappeared, to be replaced by monstrosities as in the Crystal House Syndrome, and see that their town has been filled with the sort of undistinguished architecture which makes towns all over England look the same, losing individuality and character.

The second was that 'people rather than buildings make a town great.' This is true, despite the observation above. There are no politicians, aristocrats, royalty, or mayors, Guild or otherwise, in this book. The people who do appear are Prestonians going about their daily business, playing their part in making the town 'great'. Mr Berry would not have agreed. In his two books Preston is mostly seen in the context of the powerful and the well off. He rarely touches on the lives of ordinary people.

The third was a dedication in his 'children's' history book, expressed in the florid and imperial tones of the time. He dedicated it to Preston children who 'perform their allotted tasks and are fitting themselves for a position in life's battle.' Using this as a rough base, as I may not pass this way again, I would like to make an additional dedication of this second selection to my former pupils and students in the Preston area: may they, and Preston, prosper.

John Garlington, June 2000

Tram Bridge seen from Avenham/Frenchwood, *c.* 1910. This unusual view taken from the top of the steps, on what was known as Little Avenham Brow, shows the bridge in context with the river Ribble and other bridges downstream. When the railways arrived they used a new bridge leaving this one redundant. It is a local landmark that successive local authorities have kept in good repair. It was rebuilt in the 1960s and was the only footbridge open on this stretch between 1986 and 1988.

The stone bridge in Moor Park, *c.* 1912. This postcard view by Abel Heywood of Fishergate, unconventionally for views at this time, shows the north side of Stone Bridge and purports to show a drinking fountain, apparently on the left. Apart from some very slight evidence on the stonework, nothing remains of it today. Generations of children have played on this sunken path, running under, over and clambering on it. Edward Milner built the bridge which is typical of his grotto work which is also evident on Avenham Park.

One

Uptown

Fishergate in Guild Week, 1902. Under a canopy of flags and flower swags people go about their business, behind specially erected barriers. Mixed traffic, including a hansom cab and a wagon carrying cotton goods, moves smartly along. The Corporation spent £1,059 (around £100,000 in today's money) on street decorations, including electric lights on the Town Hall spire and its Fishergate frontage and gas flambeaux illuminating the Harris Library. The area opposite, marked by the sunblinds, was to be occupied by Marks and Spencers later in the decade.

Advertising hoardings on Fishergate Hill in 1950. These hoardings, which screen the bowling greens of the Empire Services Club, seem out of place in this area of 'Victorian' prosperity and gentility. The club has its premises on Hartington Road nearby, a street of substantial Accrington brick, terraced houses built in 1900. Modern advertising boards still mark this site that was once part of an ancient area known as Spring Head Field.

Fishergate Hill at the corner of Grafton Street in 1950. Directly opposite the advertising hoardings is this building, erected in the Edwardian period and for many years the premises of Jewsbury and Brown, manufacturers of mineral water. Eventually the well-kept garden, with its neat hedges, made way for a car park. Although the building was empty at the time of writing the apple trees were still there covered in blossom.

The corner of West Cliff on Fishergate Hill in 1950. No. 24, standing proud, was once the house of William Fletcher, a man of independent means, but by the 1930s was occupied by one of William White's two butchers shops, the other being in Water Lane. On the extreme left was John Coward's Temperance Hotel, one of the longest surviving of its type in Preston. On the right is the wall of Dr Farnworth's house at 10 West Cliff Under. This was the road that the Ribble Branch Railway ran from between 1846 and 1979, emerging behind No. 24 on its way to the station.

Fishergate Hill from West Cliff corner 1910. At this time the area was inhabited by prosperous families, both professional and trade, who often also had businesses in the town. These houses, in good enough Georgian style to rival Winckley Square, lived a civil engineer, two doctors and a prosperous coal merchant with a coalyard in Fleet Street. Rebuilding has changed this view in recent times. This was probably a fairly quiet area to live until 1904 when electric trams began, stopping and starting on the spur, just visible in the centre.

Round Cliff Boys' Preparatory School in 1957. Situated at 10 West Cliff with a large garden fronting Fishergate Hill, this school flourished from the 1940s to the 1970s, run by a Mr Farnworth. Earlier a Dr Farnworth had lived and worked here. The school claimed the classes were small and 'much individual attention' was given with 'careful attention … to the development of character.' This simple Georgian style building has now gone, to be replaced by the Gothamesque headquarters of the Halifax.

Fishergate Hill at Jordan Street, c. 1914. The Commercial Hotel had had its name and purpose changed around this time from the Clarendon Temperance Hotel, one of six of its type in Edwardian Preston. The NALGO club was from the 1960s to the '70s. The area is now an open, lawned space. The cleaner stonework of County Hall clearly shows the size of the 1902-5 extensions when the building was almost doubled in size to cope with increasing municipal responsibilities, particularly concerning education. The police headquarters moved into Jordan Street as a result of these changes and are now at Hutton.

Fishergate from Butler Street, *c.* 1907. This view shows some of the variety of small businesses that existed in Edwardian Preston. The windows and signs on the right belong to a carpet dealer, a confectioner, a jeweller and the Alexandra Hotel, which boasted 'Tea and Coffee at any hour.' These properties were demolished during 1985-6 to make way for the Fishergate Centre. Across the road is the Victoria and Station Hotel alongside two cheese firms, a cycle shop and a barber's shop. This fine postcard scene by Valentine's captures some of the bustle of Fishergate.

The corner of Fishergate and Corporation Street, *c.* 1930. Turning away to the left, starting with Albert Buildings, is Corporation Street, the home of wholesale firms selling coal, timber, straw and hay, groceries and hardware. There were smaller shops also, but the general vista must have been grim with the shunting yards and the canal end with its wharf. The later was disused since 1846 and only demolished in 1938. The tram lines in the foreground are not double tracks but only part of a large spur extending to the station. Most of the system was single track.

The Theatre Royal, Fishergate in Guild Week, September 1922. The first theatre here was a plainer affair built for the 1802 Guild. In 1869 the theatre's Regency façade, designed by Ald. James Hibbert (1833-1903), was added. It was refitted in 1833, redesigned internally for the 1882 Guild and then renovated in 1898. Films were first shown there in 1911, before it became a full time cinema in 1926. It was renamed the ABC in 1959. It finally closed in 1982 and was demolished in the 1986 clearances. During the 1922 Guild, films were showing here daily at midday or at ten o'clock 'if wet'.

Fishergate near Fox Street photographed by Arthur Winter in 1935. It seems strange today to see traffic moving in both directions in Fishergate. This elevated view taken from the Theatre Royal shows how a town in the forefront of the Industrial Revolution squeezed its commercial business into a largely unchanged medieval thoroughfare. The word 'gate' is Middle English for 'street'. The streets running off it in all directions were also packed with shops, inns, banks and hotels. Lloyds Bank on the corner of Fox Street was expanded after the war and acquired its now familiar white stone facade.

Fishergate from Winckley Street, *c.* 1903. The half-timbered appearance of Burgon's grocers shop gives an idea of what Preston might have looked like today had more of the older frontages been preserved as in York or Chester. Further along from this, premises have neat, simple Georgian façades which have all been lost or altered since. Chapel Walks, marked by the white premises of Hale's tailors, is an ancient thoroughfare which skirted a warren of back lanes and yards on its way to St George's church. For many years it was a street of lawyers' offices; now it is simply the space leading to the car park.

Fishergate from the Shelley Arms (now Woolworths). The Harris Orphanage girls process along Fishergate on Whit Monday, 8 May 1905. To the right is the Gas Office, built in 1872 in the Gothic style, surmounted with a hundred foot spire. Established in 1815, Preston Gas Company supplied, in 1905, the whole district through 170 miles of pipes and 3,150 gas lamps lit the streets. To the left, formerly the main post office until 1903, is Harding's garage. Later the Kardomah Cafe was here retaining the old polished post office counter for a new use. In 1964 both buildings were demolished to provide a way into St George's Shopping Centre.

St George's Shopping Centre, Summer 1966. The pedestrian walkways and arcades on two levels, leading from the old Gas Board passage to Friargate and Lune Street, in this its first incarnation, was thought to represent the last nail in the coffin of Church Street as a commercial centre. Other factors were the establishment of stores such as C&A and the redevelopment of existing ones. St George's was opened on 22 March 1966 by Ald. Beckett and then modified and reopened in an all-covered version in 1982. A third refashioning and expansion opened in 1999.

W.S. Heane's shop in Fishergate, c. 1902. This view was published by the ill-fated Wrench Company who went bankrupt in 1906 after being outpaced by its own success. Here is an intrusion of reality, two women in shawls, which photographers sometimes tried to eliminate. On the extreme right is Heane's shop, which was only absorbed into British Home Stores in 1968. Known for its vast selection of postcards, it was regularly visited by the then curator of the Harris Museum, William Barton, to buy cards for the museum. The premises next door, now BHS, was Frederick Matthew's drapery store.

Fishergate by Glover's Court, c. 1925. On the left is the Town Hall, its Longridge stone blackened by sixty years of industrial pollution, and the Miller Arcade with its pepper pot towers, later removed for safety reasons. On the right is the white marble-fronted shop and cafe of E.H. Booth who founded his company on the site of the present Harris Museum and moved here in 1867. Booth's became famous for fine food and wines and an empire was developed in Preston and district. The high class cafe upstairs (closed in 1984) was popular and a bakery was added in Glover's Court. Since 1988 the site has been occupied by Waterstone's bookshop.

Glover's Court, 1905. Unlike its near neighbours, this was a street in all but name, though with restricted access to Fishergate. Note the spire of the Town Hall above. On the left, facing Fishergate, was George Sharples' private telephone exchange from 1879, Preston's first, which was later sold to Booth's. In 1913 full access to Fishergate was made through demolition, though Booth's maintained contact with their building by a bridge that is still there. The date of widening is shown on a plaque on the corner. This postcard, issued by J.W. Ruddock of Lincoln, reproduces a watercolour by a Lancashire artist known only as 'A.G.S.'.

Fishergate in 1824 from an engraving by Franks and Johnson. The Guild Hall, in the background, was built in 1762 and just beyond it, with its cupola showing, is the Town Hall dating from the 1782 Guild. The cupola was refashioned in 1814 to accommodate a larger clock. By 1862 both buildings had become too small for civic purposes and, being also way beyond their best, were demolished to make way for the new Town Hall. On the distant right is the parish church of St John, whose tower at this time was far smaller than shown here, having been reduced to roof level in 1810 to make it more secure.

The Town Hall and Guild Hall, Fishergate, from a drawing of 1853. Doctor Kuerden, a seventeenth-century local historian, wrote about a town or moot hall with front pillars under which were some butchers shops. The roof of this moot hall and some of its walls fell in on 3 June 1780 and a new Town Hall (this one) was erected for the 1782 Guild. Eventually thought to be too small, or not ostentatious enough, for a prospering, industrial town, the site was cleared in 1862 for George Gilbert Scott's great showpiece. The old clock ended up at Beech Grove Farm near Kirkham, where it was set into the stables wall.

The Town Hall colonnades photographed in 1953 by Edgar Blackburn. Through the massive Aberdeen marble pillars set in Longridge stone bases, can be seen the corner of Church Street and Avenham Street. The Town Hall, damaged by fire in 1947, lost its great clock tower and spire, and when the site was cleared in 1960 these pillars were ground down and now form part of the sea defences at Clifton! Across the road is the New Victoria cinema, built in the 1920s, which became the Gaumont thirty years later and the Odeon in 1963. To the left is Woods' prosperous tobacco business that enabled the family to live on Moor Park Avenue.

Church Street from the Miller Arcade, c. 1910. This is an excellent record of a once unspoilt, uncluttered group of buildings. On the left is the parish church, completely rebuilt in 1855, and to its right, at the top of Stoneygate, is the Eagle and Child Hotel, demolished in 1931. An audience watches from the balcony of the Conservative Men's Club, above the Discount Book Store. The clean line of the next block, comprises of the Bull and Royal Hotel, Snape's Printers and Church Street Chambers. The low building on the right is Addison's wine lodge, formerly the Grey Horse Tavern, from 1808 to 1854.

The Bull and Royal Hotel in an engraving from 1855. A public house called the White Bull stood here for over three centuries which was used as a dressing station for wounded Jacobite rebels in 1715. In 1745 Charles the Young Pretender, discussed plans of action here. Bought in 1773 by the Earl of Derby, an assembly room was built in Adam style with accommodation for musicians. At the rear was a cockpit used for public meetings.

The Bull and Royal Hotel yard photographed by Edgar Blackburn in 1952. The social life of the upper classes centred round the Assembly Room, which was reached down the Bull Inn court. Its window, shown above, gave a limited view of Church Street keeping the room more exclusive. Here fashionable balls were held during races week and in winter. Records exist of 'cards assemblies' between about 1775 and 1830 that were very popular, with well-to-do ladies, who arrived in sedan chairs. Accounts show that only the best candles were used and only tea was drunk.

Patronized by Their Majesties The King and Queen

BULL & ROYAL
HOTEL
PRESTON

GARAGE FOR
130 CARS
PHONES - - 2861–2
Night - - - - 318111

Banqueting Hall

ACCOMMODATION FOR DINING 300 PEOPLE

Hotel Dining Room

A Bull and Royal publicity postcard, c. 1925. The hotel has had famous guests including Charles Dickens in February 1854 who came to report the famous 'Strike and Lockout'. He visited the Cockpit to attend a workers' delegates meeting. Joseph Livesey and other teetotal reformers had held a meeting there in May 1832, establishing the Preston Temperance Society (the world's first) and subsequently rented the Cockpit from the Earl of Derby. Cockfighting continued there even after these changes. By 1880 the Cockpit doorway had been bricked up, much to the disappointment of teetotal pilgrims.

Photo by Arthur Winter, Preston

The Bull and Royal Hotel photographed by Arthur Winter, c. 1935. By the 1920s the hotel had garage space for 130 cars and catered for luncheons, banquets, dinners and weddings, describing itself as 'Preston's Old Historic Guesthouse'. On the left is the Discount Book Shop which continued into the 1970s. On the right is the balcony from which a number of Preston MPs received their supporters, notably Sir Thomas George Hesketh in 1862, an event commemorated by a painting by V.O. Sherwood.

Cheapside and the Flag Market from the Harris Museum balcony, 7 July 1913. This was almost a royal photograph! Last minute preparations are under way for the visit of King George V on the following day. The low, dark entry opposite was Castle Inn Yard and the building to its left had been The Castle Inn, opened in 1623. In 1826 it was the headquarters of William Cobbett, the Radical, who made speeches from here to political sympathisers. In medieval times the yard had been part of a thoroughfare which had run from Cheapside to Ladyewell Street and the Friary.

Cheapside, looking down Market Street, c. 1961. The far end of Market Street was created in 1893 for easier access to the markets, yet Cheapside had its own market in earlier times, around a butter cross. Here eggs, vegetables, cheese and butter were sold as well as textiles, hardware and crockery. The Preston Journal was printed and sold from here by Robert Moon from 1745. After about 1955 few original frontages survived, being constantly replaced, however, in 1959 an eighteenth-century wall of mud and straw was found.

The Flag Market from the Town Hall, c. 1904. Although now sadly very faded, this postcard illustration still shows us a wide view of the Flag Market and beyond, many years before modern street additions obscured it. On the far left is the top of Friargate which was widened in 1893. In the centre is the new General Post Office (1903) whose frontage shows how steeply the land falls away from its highest point above sea level in nearby Lancaster Road. The Covered Market and the Sessions House (1904) are on the right. The Boer War Memorial (1904) is in the centre, almost obscured by an electric tram stanchion (1904).

Market Street looking South, c. 1935. This unusual photograph shows the width and straightness of this custom built street dating from 1894-5. On the left is the end of the Fish Market and the Post Office, though looking less familiar without the row of telephone boxes. These were designed by Giles Gilbert Scott in 1935 and those put here later have since been preserved as a piece of working history. Scott's uncle designed the Town Hall, centre, and further on, the white front of Booth's can be seen. To the right are shops which replaced those hidden away in side alleys and courts.

The Boer War Memorial 6 October 1904. This photograph, taken by John Thomas Wright, who had premises on the Market Square, shows the town clerk, Henry Hamer, with the mayor and army officers, turning away after the memorial's unveiling. Serried ranks of the Loyal Regiment watch while ladies look down from the Sessions House balcony. Behind is the Cinder Pad, where the new municipal offices would be built during 1931-3. People can be seen streaming through from Lancaster Road to view the red granite obelisk which commemorates the 124 Preston dead, most of whom perished at Kimberley.

The Harris Museum and Art Gallery 1902. The museum solidly dominates, challenging Prestonians to learn and better themselves, as Ald. James Hibbert hoped they would when he designed the building and advised on its contents. On the left is the unfinished Sessions House, with scaffolding ready for the tower construction. On the right is the ornate North portico of the Town Hall from where Guilds were proclaimed from 1822 to 1952. Lancaster Road can be seen to the right and along the front is the main cab rank where two horse are eating from nosebags.

The Harris Museum and Art Gallery 1895. This early postcard photograph was issued by Wrench and Co., and shows, on the left, a view north across the rooftops and the buildings on Lord Street before demolition in favour of the Sessions House. The museum was Hibbert's pride and joy, the zenith of his career. After touring Europe viewing classically buildings he came home to erect a centre of learning and culture, which sadly led to his downfall. Incongruously, this postcard has been adapted on the obverse as a trade card advertising coal, 'Delivered loose ... cash on delivery ... bags extra .. 17/6d per ton.'

The art gallery floor of the Harris Museum photographed by J.Busby in 1930. A good example of Hibbert's attempt to 'elevate and purify the public taste' was the inclusion of three classical friezes, visible here. There is a bas-relief of an Assyrian king successful in war, a copy of a Parthenon frieze in honour of Athene, and one from the ruined temple of Apollo in Arcadia, of combat between Amazons and Greeks. Overspending and philistinism defeated Hibbert who said that 'the reference library ... and museum were left by me incomplete ...' and by 1895 work was continuing 'without any defined plan whatsoever'. He finally left Preston in 1898.

The Fish Market, c. 1905. Groups of Southport shrimpers or fishwives set up simple stalls on Earl Street or, like these, at right angles to it on the Fish Market. The Ribble had always been an ample source of fish until the 1790s when stocks dwindled through overfishing and the drawing of water for industrial purposes. Groups of fishwives came to Preston from the Fylde and down the Ribble estuary coast from Hesketh to Southport, to sell shellfish and flounders. Clad in their distinctive headgear and clothes many set off for market as early as four o'clock.

The Fish Market, c. 1905. The Covered Market is on the left and the Fish Market forms the centre of the view. It was roofed over and repaved in 1924 at a cost £6,000. It occupies an area of 100 feet by 114 feet and was, before the Market Hall opened for food sales in 1972, covered with stalls ranging from the simple to the elaborate, covered and uncovered, for four days a week. Running between the markets is Earl Street up to Lancaster Road with Preston police station on the right. In the middle area, right, two fishwives can be seen in their distinctive headgear.

The Covered Market photographed from Earl Street, *c.* 1960. Before 1875, this area was known as Colley's Garden, then Chadwick's Orchard, though the trees were cut down in 1821. The top of Orchard Street can be seen through to the left. The premises on Liverpool Street, right, were swept away for the new Market Hall in 1972, which made its first profit in 1980. As the town grew as a commercial centre for local farmers, land had to be found to expand into. This area took the overspill though other places had small outdoor markets, such as the Public Hall, until fairly recent times. From 1860 pigs were sold near Lord Street and horse fairs were held on the Covered Market.

Friargate looking South from Orchard Street corner, 1905. This is a typical Edwardian scene with a new tram, errand boy and barrow, cyclist and shops displaying their stock outside. Second from the right is R. Slinger and Sons hardware shop, which sold housewares such as kitchen ranges, patent well fires and machinery for mitreing, mortising, planing and sawing. Further on is the is the Royal Hippodrome (1896-1959), later C&A (which closed during 2000), which put on all types of entertainment, though not films. Beyond is the Hoop and Crown public house and the clock outside Thomas Yates's jewellers.

Lower Friargate photographed by George Devey, c. 1905. In progress is a Catholic Whit procession, representing the Joyful Mysteries of the Rosary. On the right is Roper Hall, erected in 1873, comprising of a school for older boys from St Mary's, the Catholic Men's Club and three shops. Its benefactors were Miss Elizabeth Roper and her sister, Mrs Maria Holland. The school closed in 1958 and Roper Hall is now a night club affiliated to the nearby Adelphi Hotel. Further along is the Sun Hotel, one of Preston's oldest inns and to its right is Back Lane, shortly to be renamed Great Shaw Street, leading to Market Street West.

Winckley Square from the south from a drawing of 1855. Lang's map of 1774 shows this area to be a large expanse of green wasteland known as Town End Field, which was crossed by a brook, the Syke, later culverted. Here, it is reputed, lived larks and snipes, only a short distance from Fishergate. This isolation appealed to its owner, Thomas Winckley who from 1807, with William Cross, laid out Winckley Square and the adjoining streets as an area for the gentry to live. On the left is the stone porticoed house of Thomas Batty Addison, a staunch supporter of the workhouse system. His house and its neighbours became part of Winckley Square Convent School from 1875.

Winckley Square from the south west, 1855. This may give the impression that the Square was open to all for strolling, but this was not the case. The 1847 Ordnance Survey map shows irregular but definite areas which belonged to the Square's residents. In the distance are the Winckley Club and Philosophical Institution, both opened in 1846. Over Cross Street is William Ainsworth's house. The Club was a retreat for rich gentlemen; the Institution was a cultural centre which became Doctor Shepherd's Library in 1868. Just visible is the statue to Robert Peel by Thomas Duckett who also decorated the Institution with heads and grotesques.

William Ainsworth's villa in Winckley Square, 1855. It is ironic that this pleasant Italianate villa, built in 1850, was the home of such a cruel, grasping and determined man as Ainsworth. Owner of a cotton mill in Cotton Court, off Church Street, he made his money from the labours of the Preston poor, fining them huge amounts from their puny wages for trifling offences. A lawyer by profession, he pursued misdemeanours, such as runaway children breaking their 'indentures', in the courts. His stylish house was demolished in 1970 and replaced by a redbrick blockhouse of offices.

The north east corner of Winckley Square, *c.* 1902. The Winckley Club and Ainsworth's villa can be seen down left [?]. On the left is No. 7, occupied by one of fourteen doctors then in the Square, later becoming the office of James Todd, who built a global accountancy empire, and became chairman of Sunbeam cars. After his death at Haydock races in 1931 his ashes were set in the office wall behind a stone plaque marked 'J.T. 1863-1931'. The gardens became more neglected after 1920 as private ownership fell, though St Wilfrid's staff attended to the upper part until Preston Council took over in 1951.

The north west corner of Winckley Square, *c.* 1912. Garden Street intersects where the horse and cart are, with the house numbers ascending to No. 33 on the right. Edith Rigby lived at No. 27, where she organised activities associated with women's suffrage. She was imprisoned and forced fed following a hunger strike. Dr Sir Charles Brown, a principal benefactor of Preston Royal Infirmary, was a doctor for over sixty years. Both had regard for their fellow humans; Edith Rigby treated her maids as her equals and Dr Brown always valued his nurses. Between 1865 and 1978, Preston Catholic College occupied all of this block except Nos 30-32.

Two

Out of Town

Egerton Road, Ashton, *c.* 1910. This luxuriantly tree-lined road runs straight in an easterly direction from Tulketh Road to Pedders Lane and the original Ashton House estate. It may originally have been a means of access for the gentry to town. Development of this road was patchy at this time though those who did live here were well-to-do such as James Askew the bookseller; Robert Simpson, a prosperous butcher in Friargate; John Enderby of Enderby and White with two drapers shops in Friargate and William Margerison, partner in Margerisons Soap Works in Leighton Street. A corner of St Michael's church, built in 1908, is visible on the right.

Tulketh Road corner, Ashton, *c.* 1910. The roads go three ways at this point, with Egerton Road to the right and further to the right, Powis Road. All this area was developed in the 1880s with widely spaced houses with gardens. From this time the new moneyed classes such as the small factory owner, prosperous tradesman or shopkeeper could afford to live around here. The writer of the postcard said she stopped at No.1 Powis Road (marked) the home of an independent lady, Mrs Alice Thomas.

Lytham View, Ashton photographed by George Devey in 1906. This building comprised three houses, one in Wellington Road occupied by a (commercial) traveller, John Toulmin and the others in Tulketh Road, then known as Nos 1 and 2 Lytham View. The latter was occupied by William Wood the registrar of births, marriage, and deaths from his premises at 29 Meadow Street, Lytham View, which has since lost its stone name plaque during renovations. There were neighbouring terraces called Sea View, River View and Pleasant View, situated down the hill towards town.

Tulketh Road, Ashton, corner of Wellington Road photographed by George Devey, 1906. Tulketh Road stretches north to Long Lane, now Blackpool Road, with new large mansion houses like Whinny-Clough, situated at the far end. The open spaces on the left were built on between the wars. The single tram track, electrified in 1904, was part of the horse tram system set up in 1882, three years later than Fulwood's, to service this prosperous suburb. On the right is 70 Wellington Road, Sacred Heart's presbytery. Mass was said in the stables of this house until Sacred Heart school was built in Poulton Street in 1904.

Wellington Road, Ashton photographed by George Devey, 1906. This is the main commercial road of the new Ashton suburb. The fashions of the time show clearly; girls in shorter, manageable dresses; the women in heavier, more restricting clothes. The church on the left is Ashton Methodist church which still flourishes. This is a street of solid, less grand housing, reflected in the solid occupations of its inhabitants - comfortable but not rich. Shops down here included a butchers, a grocers, a shoe shop and a Co-op shop opened in 1888 on the corner of Bank Place.

33

Garden Walk, Ashton, c. 1910. This road seems to live up to its name, although it has lost some of its charm today. Its inhabitants, a mixture of independents and clerical people, were the type which the 1867 Reform Act enfranchised as the town qualifications for the vote was that householders should pay rates. To the right is Prospect Place which also runs across Wellington Road. At Nos 18 and 20 George Devey had his studio from 1891, 'in the pretty suburb of Ashton … immensely better … than a skied studio in the smoke of a town.' His wife, Elizabeth, ran a servants' agency from the same address.

Rose Terrace from Newton Road, Ashton by George Devey, 1906. This was one of the most attractive corners in the maturing Ashton suburb and probably the most sylvan. The householders here were people of independent means and prosperous tradesmen. The building trade was well represented by Thomas Cottam, owner of his own firm and Robert Wilding, partner of Wildings plumbers and glass merchants, (still going strong in 2000). This postcard was sent by Mrs Margaret Kellett of 'Fentonville', to her sister's friend in Toronto to show her the house, second on the left, where they lived.

Whinny - Clough, Tulketh Road, Ashton, 1904. In 1887 land became available from the East side of the Ashton Park estate. William Park JP, a partner in Park and Sons, civil engineers and estate agents in Winckley Square, brought a plot in 1903 and built Whinny Clough, with unrestricted views all round. The picture may have been privately commissioned as this one was sent as a Christmas card by Mrs Florence Park. The building was in the Park family until 1952 and became the Tulketh Hotel in 1967. The houses at this end of Tulketh Road were known by their names only.

Lombard Terrace, Garstang Road, c. 1950. The tree on the corner of Barlow Street, long gone, gives us a clue that Garstang Road had once been a leafier place to live. Nowadays the A6 is a dual carriageway that is busy most of the time. These terraces, six in all, were built on the West side of Garstang Road in the 1860s and inhabited mainly by professional and medical people with business addresses elsewhere; that is, they lived a 'carriage ride' from town. The terraces, namely Victoria, Gladstone, Lombard, Cromwell, Alfred and Havelock were important postally and the houses were numbered within them. Road widening later took away many of the gardens.

The dedication of St Cuthbert's House, Fulwood, 1910. The congregation of St Cuthbert's church gather round as the laying of the title stone takes place in the half built St Cuthbert's House. The Revd Douglas stands second from the left. On the right is, the later to be named, Douglas Road and the buildings of the cattle market and abattoir, opened in October 1867. Before this, the market stood on the corner of Garstang Road and St George's Road where Canterbury Hall now stands.

Withy Trees crossroads from Lytham, Fulwood, c. 1930. In the foreground is Lytham Road, known as Watling Street Road West until 1913. On the left are the trees of Grasmere house, the home and surgery of Dr Arthur Dixon. Part of the land is occupied now by the modern Lytham Road Surgery. Next door was Larch House which was occupied by the McNeil family who were drapers in Church Street. Across the Garstang Road is Fulwood Methodist church, opened in 1912 with a school recently added. Double tram tracks run into Watling Street Road as a single track and using five loops that emerge as double into Deepdale Road.

The workhouse, Fulwood, *c.* 1920, no matter how pleasant the gardens may look, this is rather a grim subject for a postcard, chosen by the sender to enthuse about a 'lovely holiday'! Opened in 1868 the workhouse centralised indoor relief for Preston and district and most paupers dreaded ending up here. Families were split up when they were taken in, sometimes permanently. Men tilled the land, broke stones and picked oakum while the women sewed, knitted and cleaned. Punishment, was dished out when necessary in cells underneath. The fine imposing exterior belied the cold, plain interior, floored with store flags.

Fulwood Hall Lane, Fulwood, *c.* 1930. This avenue, developed mostly between the wars, leads to Preston Golf Club which occupied the old Fulwood Hall and farm from 1903. Until the 1990s the lane led to Longsands Lane where the Continuation Hospital was and Willow Farm where Preston North End FC trained. These were swallowed up by new developments and the Lane was cut off after Melrose Avenue by Eastway, the new circulatory road. In the foreground is one of the five tramway spurs where the trams waited for others to pass, causing many complaints about noise.

Watling Street Road from Deepdale Road, Fulwood, c. 1906. This postcard view gives us a glimpse of the quiet rural nature of this rather exclusive area at this time. The houses on the right were inhabited by prosperous, professional families, yet were only a short walk away from the workhouse. Behind the camera the road continues as Watling Street Road East to Cromwell Road making the original road, before 1913, over two miles long, and straight like its namesake. The double tram tracks are a loop to allow the inner and outer circle trams to pass safely.

Watling Street Road looking East, Fulwood, 1914. By 1914 Fulwood had houses ranging from ancient cottages to the newest 'free-style', exemplified by the houses here on the left of the corner of Duchy Avenue. Described as a 'pretty suburb' in the 1930s, Fulwood may never have prospered at all. Formed as a local government authority in 1863, it survived two attempts in 1867 and 1879 to absorb it into Preston; only petitions to the House of Commons prevented this. Its population in 1851 was 1,748, growing to 3,725 in 1881. It took fifty years to double it again, showing how 'exclusive' Fulwood remained.

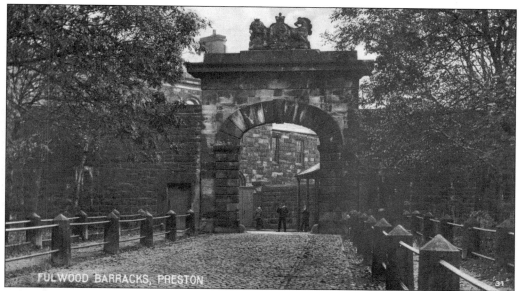

Fulwood Barracks, *c.* 1910. The barracks were opened in 1848 to house an infantry battalion, a squadron of cavalry and a battery of artillery. Later the buildings covered an area of twenty four acres and included accommodation for families. The original buildings are all of Longridge stone, as was this massive gateway, surmounted by the Royal Arms of England with Lion and Unicorn. In 1914 men flocked here to volunteer and were signed up with the Loyals, the Borders, the RAMC and East Lancs. The gate was removed in the 1960s and the barracks is now an Army communication centre.

Garstang Road, Fulwood, *c.* 1920. A woman pauses outside the Fulwood Café (now flats) and looks into Victoria Road. Today this is a small commercial centre, but in 1920 there was only one shop here (a stationers), and the café on the corner of Lytham Road,. On the left are six chestnut trees, three of which survive today. In the distance is Grasmere House the surgery of Dr Dixon and Dr John Pearson who also had surgeries in Ribbleton Lane and Deepdale Road. Trees are very much in evidence, a characteristic of Fulwood as a former Royal Forest, though Withy Trees corner nowadays has hardly any.

Garstang Road, North of Withy Trees, Fulwood, c. 1920. The trees of Grasmere House shade the pavement on this quiet afternoon. Until 1825 all Northbound traffic used the old Lancaster Turnpike Road (now Black Bull Lane) from the Marsh, Water Lane, Old Lancaster Lane and Friargate. A big problem was that horse-drawn vehicles slipped dangerously on the hills in frosty weather and sometimes the mail coach failed to get through. In 1825, The Withy Trees to Black Bull section was created, straight and wide, and was maintained by the Preston and Garstang Trust until about 1860.

Kings Drive, Fulwood, 1955. When the Atherton family sold Highfield Farm (Regent Drive) in 1930 Kings Drive was one of the avenues which resulted. The houses had names rather than numbers. On the left are Studland (now No. 24) and Melrose (now No. 22) the home of Thomas Hayes, wine merchant. Other houses included Red Roofs owned by Francis Shires, a company secretary, and Atherton House owned by John O'Kane, a cattle dealer. The O'Kanes were related to the Athertons.

Highgate Avenue, Fulwood, 1906. Situated in the south west corner of Highgate Park estate, this avenue was developed just before 1900 and grew over the next decade. The houses, which were built for newly established wealthy families, all cost over £500. Building styles are mixed, though many follow the principles of Norman Shaw and his pupils MacCartney and Field. All are symmetrical, some redbrick, some roughcast, with two gables joined by a lower horizontal roof. The house on the right was owned by the Parkers, cotton manufacturers, and its near neighbour by Blacows, funeral directors.

Garstang Road near Broadway looking South, Fulwood, c. 1930. Until 1934 the Fulwood/Broughton boundary was near Yewlands Avenue, but was then pushed further North to Lightfoot Lane. On the right is Williamson's chemists and Sharples' hairdresser's, an arrangement maintained today. Further along are the petrol pumps of the Black Bull garage, demolished in 1999, and beyond is the Old Black Bull Hotel, built in 1840 and rebuilt in the 1960s. Between the wars the Dallas bus ran along here into town and could be hailed by people when needed. Broughton now starts beyond the motorway roundabout.

Nos 12-22 Vine Street, Maudlands 1950. Old streets around St Walburge's church in Maudlands have names which connect with the leper house of St Mary Magdalen set up by Franciscans, thought now to have been sent by St Francis of Assisi himself. These names, Mill Street, Croft Street and Vine Street record important facets of medieval life. These houses, built in a style unfamiliar to Preston, were put up by the railway for its employees and its ownership explains the strict uniform appearance. Both sides of Vine Street were inhabited by railway employees by 1940.

Three
Over and Above

The town centre from the air, 1920. Published and sold by Heane's of Fishergate, this may have been the first aerial view taken of the town. In the middle is the centre of the ancient town with Scott's town hall, the post office and Harris Museum. Fishergate runs across the foreground with Cheapside, Birley Street and Lancaster Road running off it. Friargate stretches to the left and the markets, covered and uncovered, lie close to Starchhouse Square beyond. Notice how tightly the buildings are packed into this small area.

The town centre from the north, 1952. It would not have been possible to take a photograph of the Victorian centre looking like this for much longer! In the left foreground is the Orchard Methodist church followed by the markets, the post office and, to its left, the municipal offices, opened twenty years earlier. To the right of the 'Harris' are the blackened, damaged remains of Scott's town hall, to be demolished eight years later. The Empire and Ritz cinemas are on the left and in the distance stretch the streets of Avenham, such as Pleasant Street, Oxford Road and Brunswick Street, with St James church in their midst.

West of town centre, 1955. Fishergate Hill runs across, becoming Liverpool Road on Penwortham Holme where Buffalo Bill's Wild West Show performed in 1904. Broadgate is lower right and Strand Road stretches up left to English Electric. The large space on Hartington Road, on which the Electricity Board built later, is skirted by the Ribble Branch Railway, occupied here by a freight train. The bowling greens of the Empire Services club can be seen, and beyond lie the streets between Christ Church Street and Marsh Lane, clustered round Christ Church infants school.

Church Street from the town hall, 1957. Badly damaged in the 1947 fire, the town hall lost all the front portion up to first floor level and a 'deck' was created from where this photograph was taken. The Miller Arcade, left, became Arndale House in the following year and came close to demolition in 1970. Across the road is the Gaumont which became the Odeon in 1963 and at the time of writing lies empty. The public conveniences in the middle of the road have been filled in though the railings remain, now set into the pavement and preserved for posterity!

Fishergate from the *Lancashire Evening Post* office, *c.* 1955. Looking the opposite way from the previous picture, this view also shows the centre before changes took place. The white frontage on the left is British Home Stores with Heane's next door. After Guildhall Street (left) is the block including Boots and Woolworths. In the distance is the County Hall and Fishergate Baptist church. Nearer on the right is the spirelet of the Gas Board offices which were cleared away to create an entrance for the shopping centre in 1965.

St Walburge's Catholic church, Maudland, 1920. Hansom's masterpiece imposes itself on the industrial background. The church is 165 feet by 55 feet and supported by buttresses not pillars. The original roof weighed 200 tons and was made up of 7,000 pieces of timber and 18,000 square feet of boarding. The apse on the right, was created in 1873 from an original flat end. The spire is 309 feet high and is the tallest parish church spire in Britain. The parish was particularly a working class one and much of its catchment area can be seen in this view. To the left is Cocker's Moss Shed Mill and its neighbour Seeds Mineral Water factory. Beyond are the spinning houses and weaving sheds of John Hawkins on Gordon Street.

Wellington Street, Maudland, photographed by Revd Albert Williams, vicar of St Mark's, in 1952. This unusual shot overlooking Wellington Street and St Mark's church with St Walburge's in the distance. Revd Williams stood on the scaffolding at the gable end of the newly built vicarage to catch this view. St. Marks was closed in 1985 and has now been converted into flats.

Preston from the south west, 1966. This, and the following photograph, show clearly the older, established buildings now rubbing shoulders with the new, clean-looking boxes, such as Goss's (top left), Moor Lane flats (top) and St George's car park and shopping centre (right). The railway retains its ground here before rebuilding took place in Corporation Street and the goods yards gave way for the Fishergate Centre, twenty years later. Winckley Square, itself under threat as a car park at the time, is on the right.

Preston from the south east, 1966. The flats at Moor Lane and those at Avenham (bottom) seem to square up to each other over the town like boxers. Equidistant from both, in the centre, is the perhaps the most unpopular building in the town - Crystal House, the old town hall's replacement. The streets in Avenham (bottom left) soon to be cleared, are still intact, as are the Adelphi, North Road, and Moor Lane houses, also due to be demolished. Churches can be seen in this ancient 'Priests' Town'. St James's is close to Avenham flats and St Thomas's is close to Moor Lane flats. The parish church and St Walburge's are clear, though St Peter's seems tucked away in Adelphi. Mills can be seen on Brook Street, namely Arkwright and Springfield, Hawkins on Gordon Street and in the distance, the regal Tulketh Mill in Ashton. Massive immigration into Preston for work (the population reached 117,000 by 1911) produced densely overcrowded areas around the centre while the better off moved out to the new suburbs.

Four

Making Our Way

The Flag Market in, perhaps, 1868. With a certain amount of artistic licence, this engraving shows the Flag Market on a quiet day, looking more like a piazza in a fashionable town where poverty never intrudes. The house on the right is, today, Thomas Yates's jewellers and was then the house of the town surgeon, Dr Wortton in the 1680s. On the left are buildings later replaced by the Harris Museum and the Miller Arcade. These appear tiny next to the oddly proportioned new town hall with a smaller spire than Scott eventually decided upon, so that its clock could be seen from the station.

The Covered Market by Charles Edward Shaw, *c.* 1880. The town hall spire towers above all, showing how it dominated the town. Market day is in full swing with all types of people represented, rich and poor, including a blind figure on the left giving, perhaps, a more authentic view of the town than the previous picture. In the background is New Street which is where the post office now stands. The only items still remaining today are the pillars supporting the market roof. All the buildings here were demolished in 1892, making way for Market Street.

The Covered Market and Liverpool Street photographed by D.G. Cranston, 1952 . In the background is the Orchard Methodist chapel, built in Gothic Revival style in 1862, replacing an earlier church. Revd J. Guttridge was its first minister and a chapel is named after him on Deepdale Road. The chapel was closed in 1954 and its site, and those adjoining it, are now occupied by the Market Hall. The roof is held up by cast iron supports all inscribed with '1875' and Thomas Allsup's name; he re-roofed this place after the first roof had collapsed suddenly on 5 August 1870.

Horrockses cotton mill, New Hall Lane, *c.* 1860. Although spinning and handloom weaving had been done in the town since earliest times, the cotton industry was first established in Preston as a factory system in 1777. The first factory master of note was John Horrocks who built four mills between 1791 and 1802. The transition from handloom weaving to power loom weaving was slow and Horrocks built some handloom sheds in and around 'New Preston' as New Hall Lane had some become known.

Horrockses and New Hall Lane at night, *c.* 1950. In New Hall Lane, as in other districts of the town houses were quickly built, sometimes too quickly, around each mill as it was established. The Horrockses empire grew but the founder died suddenly in 1804, leaving the firm to his brother Samuel, who made his home at Lark Hill House. Thomas Miller of Bolton became a partner and the company went from strength to strength. New Hall Lane was also famous for its pubs and having a pint of beer in each pub was a famous challenge at one time. There were thirteen pubs there in 1900.

Horrockses cloth warehouse 1913. *The Preston Chronicle* of 16 June 1820 reported that a chimney, 'the highest....in the Kingdom, has been completed at the works of Messrs Horrocks, Miller and Co., near Church Street in this town. The perpendicular height from the base is 137 feet. It is intended to bring into this chimney smoke generated at ... the fires of these extensive works. This measure will remove ... the inconvenience ... from smoke thrown into the atmosphere at a low level.' If only this had been true!

The Cut Lookers at Horrockses, 1913. This was an examination room where faults in the weave were picked out. As a result of these checks the weavers would receive financial penalties or rewards for the standard of their work. From early times Horrocks powered his mills with steam engines and helped through his encouragement and customs, a pair of engineers named Richard Riley and John Paley who established a foundry in Heatley Street and built engines for others.

Horrockses weaving shed at Centenary Mill, 1920. By the time Centenary Mill was completed in 1895, the mill complex extended down New Hall Lane and across Stanley Street. Multistorey spinning shops were at the centre of a huge classically, one-level weaving shed. Massive lodges of water were needed for power. This vast industrial estate had its own generators, gasworks and railway.

Horrockses weaving shed, 1955. Despite industrial problems during 1820-30, the Great Strike and Lockout in 1853 and the cotton famine 1862-4, Preston remained a centre for cotton working, though during the quiet period 1870-80 other trades like engineering were also embraced. Horrocks[e?] produced cotton goods form 200,000 spindles and 3,170 looms in 1880. After the First World War came a decline for British cotton goods as cheap labour in the Far East undercut British manufacturers. Despite this cotton mills and their operatives still dominated in 1922 Guild Trade Procession.

Horrockses dispatch office, 1955. By 1930 factories had begun to close but over 25,000 people were still employed in cotton and Preston mills occupied eight stands at the Cotton Exhibition at White City, London in February 1931. At this time Horrockses had over 6,000 employees operating 330,000 spindles and 8,469 looms. By 1955 the operation had been reduced but the firm still sold goods all over the world. By 1952 only sixteen mills walked in the Guild Trade Procession and only eleven in 1972. Both parades included staff from Horrockses.

Horrockse's ring spinning frames, 1955. The firm was bought out in 1960 and most of its premises were closed two years later as cheap cloth swept into the country. Centenary Mill changed hands many times and now lies mostly derelict. In 1997 Prince Charles lent his name to a project that would raise money for Deepdale and turn the mill into the Millennium Mill, a centre for manufacturing, marketing and retail of textile goods. The bid for £20 million realised only £6 million which went to Deepdale. In the early weeks of 2000 locals and councillors called for Centenary Mill's demolition, even though it is a Grade 2 listed building.

Brookhouse Mill, Old Lancaster Lane photographed by J.T. Swarbrick in 1952. These are the premises of J. & A. Leigh, one of the foremost cotton manufacturers in the town. Beyond are the chimneys of Shelley Road Mill and Progress Mill (also owned by Leighs). In the 1880s Leighs employed 1,000 people working 1,156 looms and 40,720 spindles producing goods like cambrics, muslins, voiles, and organdies. By the 1930s they had 2,660 looms working and despite competition from cheap imports, Brookhouse Mill worked until 1970. Since 1979 it has been the home of Plumb's furniture covers but the 120 feet high chimney has gone.

Manchester Mill, New Hall Lane photographed by Edgar Blackburn in 1952. An empty beam is being hoisted aboard into the weaving mill's warping section. Built in 1865 among a crop of new mills in the district like India Mill, J.R. and A. Smith Ltd., wove brocades, satins, corduroy and velvets which may have accounted for their longevity as they were still working in 1979, though their original engine was stopped in 1958. The last working textile mill at the beginning of the year 2000 was the Alliance Works in New Hall Lane.

Red Scar near Preston in 1920, the future site of Courtauld's factory. During penal times Catholics worshipped and attended Mass where they could and one of these places was the Holy Well of 'Boilton Spa' at Red Scar, which was reputed to have medicinal qualities. This survived the building of the house and was removed in the 1850s. The house itself had some Elizabethan elements and its decoration was copied onto the exterior of more modern extensions.

Red Scar, c. 1855. One of the advantages of living here was the tremendous view of the bend in the River Ribble from Nab Wood to Boilton Wood. One of the proponents of Winckley Square, William Cross who lived in the first house built, actually 7 Winckley Street, also had a residence at Red Scar. He was fond of the this countryside and spent his weekends there, attending Grimsargh church on Sunday mornings and crossing by boat to attend Samlesbury church in the evening. When he married in 1813 he took up permanent residence here.

Red Scar near Preston 1922. Ironically it was water which was the house's downfall as it stood on large artesian wells, a fact which made it attractive for Courtaulds who sent in Douglas Walton of Bretherton to divine for water with a hazel rod. The site was bought and the house torn down to make way for the factory. All that remains now is a stone which once belonged to the house's observatory.

Courtauld's factory, Red Scar, c. 1950. Work began building the new factory in 1933 and was mostly complete by 1939 and occupied 150 acres. Courtaulds made Viscose Rayon yarn and water was needed for the process, so five boreholes were sunk, four of which were over 800 feet deep, to enable 50,000 gallons of cold water to be pumped out an hour. It was the largest single unit the firm had built and it brought much needed employment to the town at a time of decline in textile working.

High tenacity rayon tyre yarn manufacture, 1966. By April 1938 £2 million had been spent and the factory's two huge chimneys became landmarks. Production in 1939 amounted to 4.3 million pounds of viscose yarn, rising to 10.2 million in 1940. Soon two thousand people worked there and the figure rose to 3,500, working round the clock, by 1968. The company produced fabrics for clothes and furnishing, as well as tyre yarn for the world's motor industry.

Courtaulds, Red Scar, from the air, c. 1965. A slow recession began to bite in 1979 and Courtaulds laid off 370 workers in September that year and then closed completely in Novemeber causing 2,700 redundancies. Central Lancashire Development Corporation bought the deteriorating building in 1982 for £1.6 million and turned it into an estate of small industrial units. The underground tanks were eliminated, the railway cutting was filled in and the two 350 feet high cooling towers were taken down on 3 March 1984. By April 1984 thirty units were open. Nowadays Red Scar and Boilton Woods are conservation areas.

Victoria Quay, Preston Dock, c. 1868. By the time this engraving was made the riverside quays were very busy but a non-tidal dock was needed. Nothing was done to provide this facility and by the late 1870s trade was much reduced. Preston had been a port of sorts since about 1360 and ships, mostly small, had carried flax and timber into a sheltered harbour near Penwortham Hill. The main problem had been that the Ribble silts up easily, which was pointed out by the town doctor, Richard Kuerden who wrote in 1682 that 'the river below is much choaked up with sand.'

Preston Dock, 1955. By the 1830s, owners were not happy to risk their larger draught vessels in the dock and many river pilots refused to travel the fourteen miles from Lytham. Trade was affected and many river widening schemes failed. Finally, in 1883 the Corporation bought land and built the present dock, which was completed with a forty acre basin and a deepening of the river and its eventual diversion. Ald. James Hibbert, and a section of ratepayers, opposed the scheme saying it was 'speculative adventure that was never likely to pay … one that the Corporation should have never embarked into'.

Preston Dock, South Side, photographed by W.S. Garth in 1952. The dock was opened with great ceremony by the Duke of Edinburgh who sailed up in a steam yacht cutting a blue ribbon. Salutes were fired, crowds cheered and four hundred guests lunched in the Public Hall. The Dock made an immediate profit and became a leading importer of woodpulp for East Lancashire paper mills, China Clay, timber from Canada, Russia and Burma, grain and, from 1912, petroleum products.

Unloading woodpulp at Preston Dock, 1955. By 1902 the port's traffic had doubled, but it was reported in 1907 that, 'the shifting sands at the river mouth are a drawback.' Two years later trade slumped because the estuary had become overwhelmed with sand. After a great dredging operation was started, a new optimism for the dock grew. Year after year the town's official handbook proclaimed the dock's advantages and wealth of resources. The new Dock Offices were opened in 1936. A local historian writing in 1962 expressed the hope that the dock would soon be booming.

Preston Dock, 1955. A cargo of bananas arrive in the SS *Windward Islands*. Bananas from St Lucia and Dominica in the Windward Islands were among the new imports at this time and two vessels were built (including the one above) specially for that trade. Improvements were made to the dock including the instalment of eighteen electric and twenty three diesel/petrol mobile cranes. Four, two-ton forklift trucks and two coaling hoists were bought.

Preston Dock : roll on/roll off – Preston and Ireland Ferry Service, 1955. The dock pioneered the 'roll on/roll off' road traffic service which enabled heavy good vehicles to be driven on and off vessels through their sterns. The port authority installed a further two fifteen-ton cranes for handling deck cargo and six more thirty-two ton cranes for heavy trade from Ireland.

The *Christiane Oldendorff* bringing timber from Canada with tugboat *John Herbert*, 1965. Despite improvements, both material and financial, failure looked likely. Apart from the early period the dock had noever lived up to expectations and by 1979 it was making an annual loss of £500,000. Motorways had taken some trade and Preston could not compete with deepwater ports. Kuerdon and Hibbert had been right; by 1975 dredging was costing £600,000 a year. It was inevitable that the dock should close and eventually it did so by an Act of Parliament in 1981.

Preston Co-operative Society's North Road Store, 1902. A few Preston men tried to start a co-operative society in the town in 1862 but failed. A second attempt was made in 1869 under the name of Newhall Lane Society and made a success of its shop in Geoffrey Street. With encouragement from Mr and Mrs Outram, millowners, the venture blossomed and a second shop opened in 1873 in Adelphi. The first supply of butter was brought from the market by two society women and by 1880 the society was selling five tons a week.

Preston Co-operative Society's Central Stores, Ormskirk Road, 1902. Despite initial suspicion from some quarters the society soon began building shops in the most populated areas offering goods at competitive prices and giving a dividend. By 1905 there were twenty-two Co-op shops in Preston selling a full range of foodstuffs. Together with the Central stores, built in 1895 with extensive additions in Ormskirk Road, the society by 1914 was making sales of almost £300,000 a year and paying a dividend of £50,000. The new central offices were opened in 1909.

Preston Co-operative Society, Moor Lane Works, 1902. The society strongly supported education, at a time when the school leaving age was twelve, and ran classes in their own reading rooms, the Harris Institute and Victoria Technical School (now the university). Local charities were also supported, including the Infirmary and schools for the handicapped, to the tune of £12,000 each year. The Moor Lane Works were completed and opened in 1891.

Preston Co-operative Society Field Day, 9 August 1902. Every Summer massive field days were held when as many as 15,000 people turned out. Valuable additions were made to the organization such as Crow Tree Farm in Cadley, a furnishing departments in Lancaster Road and warehouses, abattoirs and stables in Moor Lane. Coal departments were set up at Deepdale and Corporation Street and an office at Maudland sidings bought the coal direct.

Preston Co-operative Society's Marsh Lane Store, 1902. By 1905 customers could buy almost anything from the Co-op which competed with all the big grocery businesses in town. The Marsh Lane shop, typical of all the shops, with butchery and grocery departments, was opened in 1886 to replace a smaller shop in Gerard Street. Twenty years later, with many men away in the First World War, Preston women began to be taken on by the society. The author's grandmother, Ann Anderton (later Myerscough) was employed at Marsh Lane and was the first woman to be employed by the Preston Co-op.

Church Street, looking West, 1902. The parish church spire is just visible looming out of the early morning mist over one of Preston's former shopping centres, Church Street. Workmen make alterations to the shopfront of Church Street Drug Stores on the corner of Nile Street. The hat shop of J. Eaves and Co. is next door. At one time just about every item or service could be bought in this street but after 1960 Fishergate took away much of its custom and St George's Shopping Centre took the rest from 1965. Some attempts have been made to revive fortunes here recently.

Drydens Ltd, Grimshaw Street, 1922. The massive foundry buildings in Grimshaw Street were the original works of Clark and Charnley Ltd, taken over in 1869 by William Dryden whose firm worked on until the 1990s. The site was self-contained with iron forges, brass forges, drawing offices and machine shops for turning and planing. Drydens in their early period produced axles, wheels for vehicles like trains, hoists, pulleys and hydraulic lifts. Later in their operation the firm became electrical engineers.

Dick, Kerr Ltd, Strand Road, 1922. Formed by W. Dick and John Kerr, this engineering firm took over a carriage building concern in Strand Road in 1898 employing about seven hundred men producing electric trams. Between 1898 and 1940 they produced 8,350 trams. The absorption of related concerns transformed the firm into English Electric, making aeroplanes and munitions in wartime. By 1918 the firm employed 2,000 men. They diversified into all types of electrical generation and lighting and later diesel engines.

Joseph Foster and Sons, printers engineers, 1922. Founded by Joseph Foster in 1860, this firm was world famous by 1900, working from Bow Lane Ironworks and employing about 500 men. The firm made tunnelling carriages, newspaper web printing and folding machines and lithographic and letterpress machinery. Later, operations moved to their Greenbank premises and in 1935 they were bought out by Gross Brothers of Chicago. After the war new factories were built where 1,200 worked and today Gross Graphics remain world famous as Fosters themselves once were.

Powell's Biscuits, Moor Lane, 1900. Thomas Powell established his firm in 1837 and by 1900 was a large employer producing all manner of biscuits including what they claimed was the 'Original Fig Roll Biscuit'. At this time their premises in Moor Lane extended across Ashmore Street, Vernon Street and Castle Street and had factories also in Manchester, Glasgow, Birmingham and Hull. The above building still exists though Powell's finished trading in the 1960s.

An advertisement for R. Slinger and Son, Ironmongers, 1902. Slinger's had their main shop in Friargate next door to the Black Horse Hotel and their showrooms and machine shops in Corporation Street. Both premises had telephones in 1900, which was unusual for the time. Their range of stock was extensive to say the least. The above advertisement covers only a part of what they offered; other more prosaic examples advertised fireplaces, hearths, boilers, copper cylinders, baths, lavatories and mantels. Slingers survives today and trades from Paley Road.

Flatts Mill, Walton-le-Dale, c. 1965. William Calvert and Sons owned two mills in Aqueduct Street and Walton-le-Dale and by 1880 were producing cotton goods from 150,000 spindles and 2,500 looms with 2,200 operatives. Nine boilers drove four engines for power and a new engine house was built in 1899. The taller of the two chimneys, 180 feet tall, was built in1885. Between the wars Calverts went out of business and its premises were then used by Ribble Paper Mills from 1935 until about 1980.

Seed's Mineral Waters, Kirkham Street, from a drawing by Edwin Beattie in 1896. Tucked away in an advertisement is this engraving by Preston's famous artist. His unusual eye for detail makes this picture much more than an advertisement: beyond the factory one can see the main London to Glasgow railway, houses on Maudland Bank and the terraced houses in Maudland, all dominated by St Walburge's church. The proprietor of the works, William Seed, lived round the corner from the works, next door to St Peter's School in Cold Bath Street.

Five

Beyond Our Sight

North Road, 5 September 1922. This was a red-letter day for those walking here as English Martyrs; their church, was celebrating its 55th anniversary that day and they were participating in the Preston Guild celebrations. The church can be seen in the distance, looming centre, over the roofs and is the only building from this scene remaining in 2000. Everything else, including the Brackenbury Cinema (left), was demolished in the 1960s.

St Vincent's Orphanage, Fulwood, *c.* 1910. In the tradition of Victorian Catholic life in Preston, the money needed to build St Vincent's was raised by a week 'long bazaar' in 1891 at the Public Hall that made £7,000. The orphanage was opened in 1896 and catered for the welfare of 300 pauper Catholic children between three and fourteen years.

The Dining Room in St Vincent's Orphanage, *c.* 1910. Across Garstang Road, the Harris Orphanage was organised around smaller house units, but St Vincent's boys were put in large dormitories. Their brass band was famous for miles around and the boys were also taught practical skills. At fourteen years, they left and went to live in the St Vincent's Hostel in Deepdale while seeking work. In 1956 St Vincent's became a day school before closing in 1960. It was demolished during 1963.

English Martyrs' school, Garstang Road, 1975. English Martyrs' church was built in 1867 to serve the families who lived in the terraced houses that clustered around the mills in Southgate, Moorbrook Street, Moor Lane and John Hawkins Ltd in Gordon Street. The parish also stretched north into rural Fulwood. A school was built in 1871 for 500 pupils but was found to be to small within five years. In 1869 the parish numbered about 7,000 people.

Teachers and pupils of English Martyrs' boys school, Garstang Road, 1922. In 1876 new schools were built on this site large enough to educate over 1,300 pupils and the Sunday school was held here with nearly 1,000 regularly attending in 1902. School boards, set up for state schools in 1870, were swept away when responsibility for schools passed to the local authorities. Parishes could not hope to cover the soaring costs of education and welcomed their new 'voluntary-aided' status.

English Martyrs' schools ready for demolition in 1975. By 1920, the schools had become overcrowded again and a new school was built for the boys in Berkeley Street. By 1975 this was the last, single sex primary school in the town. In 1936 the poor condition of one wall in the girls' school meant that they had to go to the boy's school for a while. The hours were staggered to accommodate the extra numbers. In 1972 significant deterioration of the building led to the school's final downfall – literally!

English Martyrs' schools', 1975. This was the former infant's playground, with floor boarding being stripped out prior to demolition. Beyond is the door which led to Miss Hall's classroom. Miss Hall, known in the parish by her married name, Mrs Hurst, had returned during the war under her maiden name, as women before the war usually ceased teaching when they married. This site is now occupied by Canterbury Hall.

English Martyrs' church and school, 1975. This is a picture of contrasts; the school looks dark and dilapidated and was about to be demolished while the church stands out with its light, Longridge stone cleaned of a century of grime for the 1972 Preston Guild. The parish size was reduced gradually; in 1924 Deepdale went to St Gregory's and Fulwood went to St Edward's (1943) and St Anthony's (1944). Extensive demolition in the area between 1963-5 and 1982-5 reduced it even further.

English Martyrs' boys' school, Berkeley Street, May 1972. On 13 December 1926 all the boys at English Martyrs' picked up their chattels and walked down Aqueduct Street to their new school with Mr Reeves, the head and his staff. Among the new staff was Bob Garlington (the author's grandfather) who came as 'supply' and stayed until 1962. There were 420 pupils in 10 classes ranging from eight to fourteen years. In 1958 there were 450 boys but numbers dwindled with the building of new secondary schools. St Thomas More (now Corpus Christi) took all the seniors in 1965. There were 140 junior pupils in 1972.

English Martyrs' boys school, Houghton Shield Winners, 1934. For almost all of its existence the school was renowned for its sporting prowess, especially in football and cricket. Trophies, like the coveted Houghton Shield were won against fierce opposition from other schools. This team excelled itself with one of the boys scoring a century at West Cliff. Their teacher was Bob Garlington (top left). The school hall was used for parochial activities like dances and before 1940 the yard was used by the parish tennis club. The school left this building in 1975.

John Hawkins Ltd under demolition, May 1972. Across Moorbrook Street from English Martyrs' boys school was the mighty cotton factory of Hawkins Ltd, a huge industrial complex and employer of many from the local streets. After the factory was cleared away plans were already laid to build a new English Martyrs' primary school in its place.

Demolition of John Hawkins Ltd, May 1972. John Hawkins built Greenbank Mill near the then open running Moor Brook in 1836. On February 27, *The Preston Chronicle* stated 'on the top of the brow an extensive mill is being erected by Mr Hawkins - the bricks made and burnt on its very site and the lodge almost already formed by a natural hollow in the hill.' By 1880, at their smaller factory in St Paul's Road (Little Hawkins) and here (Big Hawkins) over 1,500 operatives worked 1,900 looms and 95,000 spindles.

Hawkins shop 161/2 Friargate 1967. This shop, situated next to C&A, was one of sixty one Hawkins shops nationwide which, by this time, were owned by William Birtwistle Ltd. Birtwistle's also ran eleven mills in Central Lancashire, including the two Hawkins factories. A strong attempt was made in the late 1960s to push back cotton as a flexible, fashionable textile but this was largely unsuccessful and despite success with its staple items like sheets, towels, overalls and skirts, the mill closed in 1971.

Nos 5 and 7 Ellen Street, May 1972. Running parallel to Aqueduct Street was Ellen Street. The arrangement of the doorways at this the East end show the houses to have been built after 1875 - the lobby giving common access to two backyards and the distinctive 'Prestonian ears' over the doorway lintel. The need for backyard toilets has been removed by the conversion of the front bedrooms into bathrooms. A century ago these houses were occupied by well-placed cotton operatives. Ellen Street almost totally disappeared during the demolitions of 1983-4.

Aqueduct Street, looking west, May 1972. This street, which runs as a continuation of St George's Road, down to Fylde Road, was so named because of the small aqueduct near Shelley Road which carried the Lancaster Canal. It was lined with a mixture of buildings; industrial, terraced houses, built after about 1875, and smaller contractors' yards, such as can be seen in the distance on the left. After the demolitions of 1983-4, no houses were left on this stretch and another urban street gave way to industrial and retail units.

Heysham Street, 31 August 1916. Today completely empty of houses, Heysham Street runs parallel to Adelphi Street. Originally its dwellings were the older type with round-topped doorways. They were small with large backyards and with access by a lobby. This is the funeral cortege of Pte William Young VC who lived at No. 7 moving away, escorted by a detachment of the East Lancs Regiment. He had won the VC in France saving his wounded sergeant but died a year later on the operating table. He is commemorated in English Martyrs' memorial chapel.

Demolition of Brookfield Mill, Southgate, 31 May 1986. One of several mills in the area, Brookfield took its water for power, like other mills, from the deeply culverted Moor Brook. Built for John Liver in 1842 the mill soon became surrounded by small terraced houses and produced, for much of its time, curtain material and carpets. The Livers left in 1950 when cheap oriental produce was flooding the British market. Closure came in 1964, partial demolition in 1982 and final loss in 1986. A B&Q store stands here now.

North Road, west side, c. 1952. North Road, one of the older throughfares in Preston and one of the earliest tram routes, was fronted by private and commercial premises in equal measures. Just in the view at the left is part of the large North Road branch of the Co-op. In the centre are No. 229, recently changed to a bakery from a tripe shop, and No. 231, Mrs McConnell's temperance bar, one of seven such bars in the town. This stretch ran from Aughton Street to Fish Street and the whole lot was demolished in 1964-5.

North Road, east side, c. 1952. The houses on the left are examples of Preston's older housing stock with rounded doorway tops. The street opposite is Brownlow Street and all those houses were parallel to St Ignatius's Square, which ran behind them. Joseph Traynor cut hair at No. 182 for many years while Gaythorne's leaded lights shop traded under the name of Gayhomes. This view shows again the diversity of building use in this area before its demolition in 1964.

North Road, east side, *c.* 1952. The three houses here are Nos 347, 349 and 351, the middle of a block of nine houses that ran from the junction of Lancaster Road and North Road (left) down to the junction with Moor Lane (right). Evidence of this can be seen in the merging of two sett patterns in the road. This block, and the surrounding streets, were built in about 1840 for workers in the mills that relied on the Moor Brook for power. The street's gradient, visible in the photograph, shows a decline into the valley of that now culverted water course. In the top left corner is the blackened spire of St Thomas' church.

St Thomas's church, Lancaster Road, 1982. After the demolitions of the 1960s St Thomas's stood out more clearly as a landmark, as seen here from North Road. Built in 1837 in mock-Norman style, it was one of four churches built to provide for the growing town. The parish numbers were too great to be accommodated by 1872 and a chapel/Sunday school was built. Also by 1872 a full system of schools was in progress with over 900 pupils attending. Decline came with the clearances and the church closed in 1983, becoming a leisure and recreation centre for Age Concern soon afterwards. Sandblast cleaning revealed its light stone again for the 1972 Guild.

North Road east side, near Bradley Street, 1950. This road was a mixture of houses and shops in roughly equal proportions. The fish and chip shop at No. 287 was one of six and there were two pawn shops, one on Bradley Street corner. In the distance to left is the massive Co-op Stores. In 1900 there were twenty two grocers shops and twenty three public houses (down to fourteen by 1950). In 1950 there were eleven hairdressers and nine newsagents and several confectioners and tobacconists. It seems also to have been a centre for furniture shops for a long period. There were ten in 1900 and still eight in 1950.

St Augustine's church from Avenham flats, 1964. Practically everything in this photograph has now gone or been radically changed. The streets running parallel the camera, Hudson Street, Gorst Street and Oxford Street were demolished soon after this, as was St Austin's Club (left) behind that is the Larkhill Convent School (now Cardinal Newman College) and in the centre is St Augustine's church and presbytery. On the far right are the Ribble Offices (later Telewest cable TV) and beyond (just visible) is Ribble paper mill's chimney.

St Augustine's church, c. 1855. This church, the first Catholic church in Preston to be staffed by secular priests, was built to minister to the town's growing population. Notable Catholic gentlemen met in 1836 in the Shelley Arms in Fishergate to discuss finances and work began in 1838. The church was opened in 1840. The speed of construction was remarkable, even by today's standards, but reflects, perhaps, how much it was needed. The town's population increased from 45,000 in 1838, to 51,000 in 1841 and 85,000 in 1870.

St Augustine's church, c. 1910. The new church, with fields and meadows at its back and a maze of streets to its front, was smaller and less ornate than it was to become later. A growing attendance, 3,000 on most Sundays, necessitated alterations and enlargements that were completed in 1879. The Golden Jubilee extensions in 1890, included the refashioning of the great Ionic portico and the construction of two seventy feet tall towers with distinctive cupolas, which cost £6,000. The building, now disused, may become part of a community project after 2000.

St Augustine's interior, *c.* 1910. The church never had pillars but the weight of the ceiling, which was a barrel vault covered with sunken panels, was supported by pilasters. The 1960s demolitions reduced parish numbers and the church itself began to suffer structural problems. After redecoration and changes to the sanctuary, pieces of the ceiling began to fall, revealing dry rot infestation. In 1984 the church was declared unsafe and is no longer in use.

St Augustine's church from St Austin's Road, *c.* 1960. On the left is the Morning Star Inn which stood at the corner of Park Road. Further on the left is St Augustine's boys' school which had a frontage in Charlotte Street. The entrance to St Augustine's Club (hidden by the telegraph pole in this view) is on the right. The men's club was upstairs and there was a dance hall downstairs. The little girl is standing on the corner of 'Little' Charlotte Street and Cuerden Street is beyond on the right. The author's own family, the Garlingtons, lived a few doors down from here at No. 13, from 1853 – 1873.

Vauxhall Road looking south, towards St Augustine's, in 1960. Vauxhall Road was a continuation of St Austin's Road, as it dog-legged down to Syke Hill. The low wall visible on the left fronted a small chapel where the first Mormon service held outside America is reputed to have been held in 1837. During its final years before demolition the chapel was St Augustine's boys' club room. Around 1840, the Mormons moved to Longton where they achieved a keen following for a time.

Vauxhall Road looking north, 1960. This is the east side of Vauxhall Road by the corner of Paradise Street. In the distance is the confluence of this road and two other streets, Walton Street and Syke Hill, near to Stoneygate. The first five houses on the right are handloom weaving cottages. They had cellar windows just above street level to let in the light for working the looms before gas or electric lighting was available. In 1830 about five thousand people depended on a home handloom weaving, many of them living in this small area of streets.

Russell Street, Avenham, c. 1935. About this time the Corporation began a housing improvement scheme, repairing older properties, fumigating (with hydrogen cyanide), adding new sanitation and, in extreme cases, demolishing properties. Eighty-four houses were cleared in the first stage, some of them in Avenham and Russell Street. In this street, which ran from Avenham Lane, opposite the gasworks and parallel to Frenchwood Street, appeared in the 1814 Census and poll books of the period. Like many others this house had shared a common back space and privies with neighbouring houses.

The National school, Avenham Lane, c. 1920. Known also as the Avenham Lane or parish church school, this establishment was built in 1814 and followed the monitorial system advocated by Andrew Bell and Joseph Lancaster where older pupils taught younger ones under the supervision of an adult teacher. Bell visited Preston in 1816 to check that the standards were being maintained. It was demolished around 1977 and low level flats now occupy the site..

The gasworks, Avenham Lane, 1920. Built in Georgian style in 1816, this prosaic, industrial building was only a very short walk away from the more stylish area of Avenham centred around Ribblesdale Place, Bairstow Road and Bushell Place. Preston was the first place to be illuminated by gas outside London and its use was promoted by the rector of St Wilfrid's, Fr Joseph Dunn. Thirty years later an extension was built, on the outskirts, in Walker Lane. Both sites are now occupied by car parks.

Syke Hill from Vauxhall Road, c. 1960. The handloom weaver's cottages on the right are in Walton Street and the next block are on Syke Hill with the parish church spire visible in the distance. Unlike the two other small watercourses in Preston, Swill Brook and Moor Brook, the River Syke, which ran along here from a spring near Queen Street to Broadgate, was culverted and used as a sewer. It was once a pleasant stream which ran through Town End Field and its valley can be traced from here down Cross Street and Garden Street.

Preston Co-operative Society's Syke Hill Store, 1900. This shop stood facing north, at Nos 7 and 8, on the corner of Albert Street. Times were hard for businesses during the trade slump between 1873 and 1879 when wholesale prices fell by twenty-five per cent. This hit the Co-op Society hard and deeds were mortgaged. Improvement came in 1880 and a temporary shop in Avenham Lane was replaced by new premises in 1883, which turned out to a good year with 2,166 members and share capital of £9,860.

St James's church, Avenham Lane, 1982. Built on the site of a Nonconformist chapel in 1814, St James's was redesigned in 1881 by the ubiquitous Ald. James Hibbert, when it acquired a tower. It was altered extensively again in 1912. Parish life was very busy the best part of a century with singing, both in the church and in music festivals, sport, Guilds and education. However, by 1983 dry rot and other problems led to closure of the church and the hall was made into a chapel. The original church was demolished some years later.

St Wilfrid's school in Fox Street, 1920. Fox Street school, as it was first known, was an expensive undertaking when it was established in 1814. The cost of the land alone at £300 was a huge consideration for the time. The money was raised, eventually, but attendance was not free. By 1821 940 Catholic children were being taught here. At times other parish schools were housed here as well until Roper's school began taking senior children in the 1870s. Education continued in Fox Street until 1998.

St Mary's RC church in Friargate, c. 1905. The carpark behind Friargate, in Simpson Street was once the site of St Mary's church which had seen many changes and threats to its existence. It was a secret Mass centre in time of persecution. It was destroyed by thuggish arsonists in 1764, closed in 1793 and reopened in 1814. There was a total collapse of the roof in 1856. Falling numbers in the parish, evident as early as 1956, and a fire in the roof followed by the discovery of dry rot in 1967 hastened its end. It served as a chapel-of-ease to St Wilfrid's from about 1960 and finally closed in 1990 to be demolished in 1994.

Cannon Street Congregational church, 1902. This photograph was taken from the corner of Guildhall Street and Cross Street (part of the Grammar School wall is visible at bottom left). When the church was opened in July 1826 the front door faced Cannon Street, hence the name. During alterations in 1887 the entrance was switched to Guildhall Street with the addition of this imposing portico. The interior, however, was said to be extremely plain. This building superseded other independent chapels in the town and was finally replaced by an office block in the 1960s.

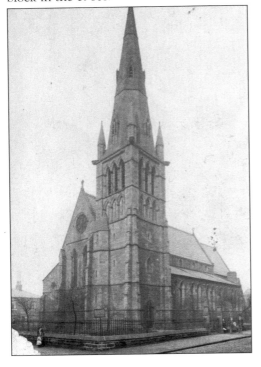

St Luke's CE church, Fletcher Road, c. 1910. In 2000 St Luke's is used by a housing association. Its parish was destroyed by housing demolition around it that was replaced by industrial and commercial units. The church opened in 1859 and its Victorian parish seems to have been a difficult one. Hewitson describes the men as liking 'ale better than their mothers' and women 'beautiful in their unwashedness'. He also noted the attendance was low - 350 out of a parish of 5,500 in 1869. There must have been some improvement as the school was expanded and there were additions to the church's fabric. It closed on 28 January 1990.

The old town hall's demolition in 1862. The town hall was hastily rebuilt in time for the 1782 [?] after its roof fell in two days after a ball had been held. Its size, or lack of it, meant that the building behind it had to accommodate the official events of the five Guilds between 1762–1842. This building, the Guild Hall, was inhabited during ordinary times and the people were turfed out during Guild celebrations. In the absence of a town hall in 1862, the official Guild opening procession came from the Grammar School in Cross Street. The following day the foundation stone of Scott's Town Hall was laid.

The back passage between Lill's Court and Union Street, 29 July 1959. The building in the distance is a neighbour of Halewood's Bookshop in Friargate. With each phase of the Industrial Revolution came an influx of people into Preston for work. Between 1811 and 1851 the population swelled from 17,000 to 67,000, the latter living in around 7,000 houses. The Catholic poor lived around Friargate, clustered round St Mary's church and in courts like this one, running down to Back Lane. Edwin Waugh, the dialect author wrote in 1867 of 'gloomy little houses', 'low narrow entries', 'pestilent vapour' and 'dark courts'.

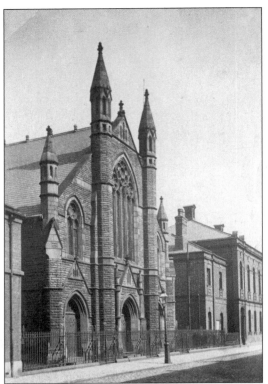

St Mary's Street Wesleyan chapel, c. 1914. John Wesley came to Preston to preach on four occasions between 1780 and 1790 to an ever-growing Methodist congregation. St Mary's Street Mission began in 1852 when the Methodists in the New Hall Lane area worshipped in rented rooms. In 1865 a school was built, with a chapel above (right). Demand grew and the chapel was added in 1885 to a basic Gothic design by James Hibbert. Attendances filled the 700 capacity building for 80 years until demolitions affected them too and the chapel closed in 1965. It is now occupied by a firm of printers.

The Star Bakery, 73 Ribbleton Lane, 1950. These premises on the corner of Almond Street were, until about 1948, the Star Hotel. It had been one of fourteen public houses on this road after the 1904 Licensing Act. The nature of the area can be gauged by the derelict shop next door which had once been a greengrocer's then a watchmaker's. The bakery shop appears to have closed although there is a delivery van parked outside. On the door is pasted a police notice with a warning about 'Wilful Damage'. The last recorded mention of this bakery is in the 1953 telephone directory. This site is now occupied by modern retail units.

Tulketh Hall, Hesketh Street, Ashton. This building has had a varied history; from 1124 it was the home of Marmaduke Tulketh, then was occupied by Savignac monks who moved to Furness and founded a famous abbey. During penal times Mass was said here in 1607 and 1153, confirmations took place here in 1687. Later it was occupied by the Hesketh family. It was a Quaker school from 1847-1855, home to the vicar of St Marks for some years and then a Brothers of Charity home for boys until about 1950. It was restored by Joseph Hansom, the architect of St Walburge's, though later he thought he had defaced it!

Isherwood's garage on Strand Road and Fishergate Hill corner, c. 1950. Still called New Bridge Garage even though the Ribble Bridge was nearly forty years old by this time, this garage had hardly changed in fifty years. In the 1970s it was transformed out of recognition and the site was eventually cleared in 1998. In the 1920s Rushton-Horisby and Daimler cars were sold here and a large placard outside read, 'To Blackpool 17 miles – Stop here for Petrol, Benzol and Oils … We have everything for the motorist.'

Troy Laundry, Lytham Road (then Seymour Road), 1900. The laundry, seen here from the grounds of St Cuthbert's church, not only offered a wide range of cleaning services but also dyed fabrics and beat carpets! The premises were extended to the left, towards the railway line, and the laundry continued to operate until about 1970. The building survives and has been occupied for much of the time since then by Tom Finney Ltd.

St Mark's CE church, St Mark's Road, Ashton, c. 1910. St Mark's and St Walburge's are close neighbours and both survived in this heavily populated area for over a century. St Mark's was opened in 1865 and its tower was added just as St Walburge's spire was also being finished. Schools were later built. An eventual fall in parish size and some decay of the fabric led to a removal to the church hall in 1983 and after a decade of sitting empty, the church is now occupied by flats.

Six
Making Inroads

New Hall Lane junction with Blackpool Road, c. 1950. New Hall Lane is to the right where the terrace is, uncompromisingly, called Cemetery View. To the left is Church Avenue and Blackpool Road runs behind the camera. Known for a time as the Arterial Road, Blackpool Road was built during 1922/4 to specifically take traffic from Yorkshire and East Lancashire away from Preston on its way to Blackpool. The increase in the number of tours by coach and charabanc had become a nuisance in the narrow town centre.

The cemetery gates, *c.* 1905. The cemetery main entrance originally stood on Hesketh Road and was opened in 1855 to relieve overworked Preston church graveyards at a time when the town had the country's highest mortality (for instance, between 1860 and 1870 nearly 14,000 Preston children died). The Arterial Road passed here in a North Westerly direction from 1922. Hesketh Road was reshaped and Illingworth and Fermor Roads were severely truncated. Tullis and Heaton Roads disappeared altogether. For about forty years, from April 1925, a Sunday bus service was run here along Blackpool Road.

Cold storage unit, Longridge Railway, Ribbleton, 1950. Moving further northwest the Arterial Road, known in this new stretch as Blackpool Road, from the start passed Ribbleton Avenue about a quarter of a mile from its translation from Ribbleton Lane. A similar distance further on was the first obstacle, the Preston to Longridge railway line on which the storage unit stands. Opened in 1850 and serving stations at Deepdale, Grimsargh and Whittingham, the line was closed to passengers in 1930 and goods in 1967. The first of three road bridges was built over this railway.

Blackpool Road looking east, 1950. In the distance is the bridge over the Longridge railway and this stretch of the road, to the junction with Deepdale road (behind the camera), was all new. On the left are the railings of the isolation hospital, opened in 1907 and closed about 1985 to be replaced eventually by Sainsbury's Superstore. St Gregory's church was built in 1936 after an earlier one (now part of the school) became too small. This quiet, leafy road was soon to change and queues of cars waiting here in two lines on their way to Blackpool would become a common sight.

Serpentine Road (now Blackpool Road) looking west, 1950. In 1883 Anthony Hewitson described Serpentine Road as 'attractive bordered with trees and for either riding or driving, very pleasant and convenient.' The Arterial Road linked up with this road at Deepdale Road and its situation changed thoroughly. On the left is Moor Park with the Serpentine and Duck Pond, further along on the right is Fulwood Park which comprises large detached houses north of Eaves Brook with allotments behind the hedges on the right.

Preston Steam Laundry on Addison Road (now Blackpool Road), 1930. This building, which stands between Emmanuel Street and Wildman Street, is no longer a laundry but houses a number of commercial ventures. Situated just over two miles from the cemetery, the building was situated on Addison Road running from Garstang Road to Brook Street. The neat gardens at the front hint at a more rural past and the pavement which took their place was much reduced in 1972 when the road was widened.

Blackpool Road, looking east from Lane Ends in 1930. In the distance can be seen the second of three new bridges necessary because of the new road. This one runs over the main London to Glasgow railway line which was opened in June 1840, very early in railway history. About 500 yards nearer to the camera is the third bridge, over the Lancaster Canal. Before this time, anyone wanting to travel to Ashton from Addison Road had to detour down Brook Street across Eldon Street railway bridge and across the canal by Roebuck Street bridge to reach Lane Ends. The chimney of Tulketh Mill is on the left.

Lane Ends, Long Lane (now Blackpool Road) looking west, *c.* 1910. From this point to Pedders Lane, nearly half a mile further on, ran Ashton Long Lane and in the distance can be seen a rise in the road which is the bridge built over the railway line to Blackpool in 1840. Before the Arterial Road came here, this stretch was a tranquil and fairly isolated community. The substantial houses on both sides have gardens, some with mature trees. The shop on the left, one of the area's landmarks, was a confectioners for many years, specialising in ice cream and iced drinks.

Clifton Terrace, Long Lane, 1905. Although the terrace exists today it is hardly recognisable from this photograph. The sylvan view made up of hedges, ivy and trees has become bleak and spartan as various widenings of Blackpool Road have deprived the houses of their gardens, making them simply spectators to the dual carriageway.

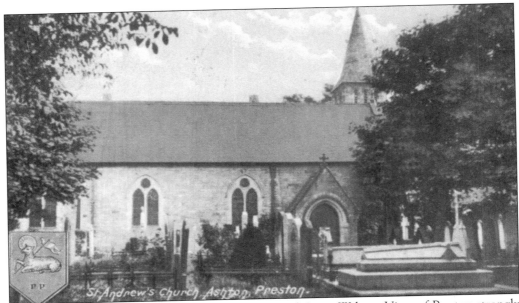

St Andrew's CE church, Long Lane, 1905. The Revd Carus Wilson, Vicar of Preston strongly promoted the founding of churches away from the town centre and St Andrews was one of these, built in 1836. It cost £2,000 and was built in the Norman style. Reconstruction of the nave took place in 1873, partly paid for by Mr E.R. Harris of Whinfield who commissioned a window to the memory of his parents. He is buried in the churchyard and in his will he left sufficient finance to pay for the Harris Museum, Harris Orphanage and to rescue what was to became the Harris 'Art College'.

Long Lane and St Andrew's CE School, c. 1910. In the distance, looking east, is the railway bridge near Haslam Park and Pedders Lane, with the end of the Arterial Road a short distance behind the camera. To the right is Tulketh Road and St Andrew's school which was started in 1866 and which was attended by 640 pupils by 1883. From the 1880s horse trams had run around this prosperous suburb and part of the system, evident in the rails in the road and stanchions holding trolley wires, was electrified in 1904.

Seven

Ways and Means

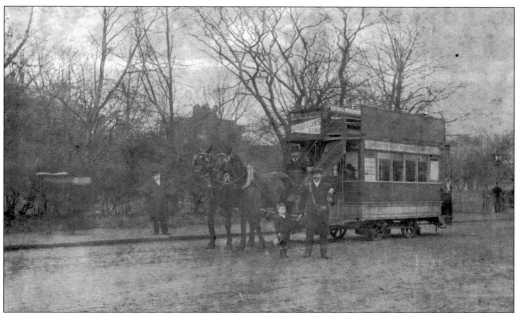

A horse-drawn tram outside Fulwood Barracks, 31 December 1903. Horse-drawn public transport began in Preston in 1879 when a horse bus service was started in Fulwood with routes in Ashton. Horse trams took over and by 1882 these were servicing Fulwood and Ashton with eight double deckers. Preston Corporation stopped the leases to the private firms who ran the service on the last day of 1903, the date written on this postcard. The town had six months to wait for the new transport system.

Tram No. 16 near the Discount Book Store, Church Street, c. 1920. This tram was one of the first electric trams used in 1904. Built by the Tramway Company in Strand Road it was powered by a 25hp motor and seems never to have had an enclosed top deck like most of its contemporaries. The gauge used by the new electric trams was 4ft 8in, over a foot wider than the horse rails. Like most trams this one had controls at each end so the driver changed ends at the terminus and only had to move the trolley's position on the overhead cable.

Tram No. 14 in Church Street near the Parish Church, c. 1920. The tram is standing outside the Eagle and Child pub which was demolished in 1931). This tramcar, like its fellows, Nos 15 and 16, never acquired a cover for its top deck, though all the other twentythree originals from 1904 did. The sign showing 'O' indicates that it is proceeding on a 'short working' which each route had. Farringdon Park had Skeffington Road and the Cemetery; Ribbleton had the 'Old England'; Fulwood Outer Circle had Moor Park, the Inner Circle the opposite side; Ashton had Powis Road and Penwortham (actually Broadgate) had the railway station.

Tram No. 13 outside the Miller Arcade photographed in 1932 by Dr H.A. Whitcombe. This tram, built in Preston at Dick Kerrs, had been supplied to Lincoln in December 1919 with others, costing £1,800 each. When Lincoln dismantled its tramway in March 1929 Preston bought three and numbered them 13, 18 and 22 replacing originals which were probably then used as a source of spares. These were important because they were designed for use under low bridges and hence were seen on the Ashton route, i.e. with Fylde Road bridge. Dr Whitcombe took 10,000 photographs of trams in the late 1920s and early 1930s.

Tram No. 22 Church Street outside the Blue Bell Hotel, 1932. By the time the Lincoln trams came back to Preston they had been fitted with vestibules round the front and were distinctive for their open balconies. Preston originals were enclosed. Just in view here is the Blue Bell, an ancient inn. In 1882 the landlord's daughter, Annie Ratcliffe, had planned to elope with her lover, John Simpson but he slit her throat in the Sir Walter Scott on North Road when they argued. In 1944 in the Blue Bell an American soldier was killed by a British soldier after some taunting about the Battle of Arnhem.

Tram No. 22 outside Miller Arcade in 1932. This is probably another of Dr Whitcombe's photographs. In 1936 he wrote a monograph on the history of trams and left his vast collection of photographs to the Science Museum when he died in 1943. As a result we have an excellent history of Preston's tram era just as it was coming to a close . On 18 January 1932 the decision was made to convert to buses. A year earlier the bus garage was extended to accommodate the new buses that were to replace the old solid tyre vehicles which, from 1920 had run to Fulwood via Plungington. Ten petrol driven buses were ordered for later in the following year.

Tram No. 31 at the junction of Tulketh Road and Powis Road photographed on 15 December 1935 by W.S. Garth. On this, the last day of Preston tram operations, this enthusiast took photographs of tramcars working their last journeys in Preston colours. Tram No. 31 was one of six single deckers bought from Sheffield in 1919 which had their fronts enclosed. Attempts to build an upper deck on these models failed. They usually worked the Ashton route. Critics of the trams pointed to certain areas of track which needed drastic repair, namely the Ribbleton and Farringdon Park routes.

Removing the train tracks from outside St Peter's church, Fylde Road, winter 1936. The men in the foreground are replacing the setts while further ahead a rail can be seen still in place. The new estate at Greenlands was serviced by bus from 1931 and Farringdon Park in July 1932, making six routes in all. Twelve trams were sold in 1933 and Ashton became a bus route in 1934. Twenty four new buses were bought in 1935 and the trams were withdrawn without any official commemorations. Corporation workmen removed the Preston tracks at a cost of £11,300. Fulwood's tracks were removed by county workmen.

Fishergate, 1937. It looks a strange sight now to see a bus driving *up* Fishergate as the traffic has been one way only along here for over thirty years. The road setts show evidence of recent resetting where the tram tracks were removed and the stanchions which formerly held up trolley wires are still in place. The bus, No. 54, was built at Leyland with an English Electric body and was in service from 1933 to 1950. The old *Lancashire Evening Post* offices are on the right.

Moor Nook town centre terminus, Birley Street. Most of the town centre terminuses were clustered around the Harris Museum, where hansom cabs and others had had their ranks, and the Miller Arcade. This area was often lively with buses, as in the photograph, which is such a contrast with today's partly pedestrianised area. Bus No. 88 was of Leyland origin and was bought in 1946 in a batch of six that worked for twenty-seven years. Moor Nook was the last new service before the war (July 1939) and was known as Moorside until 1952.

Cheapside, *c.* 1955. A shiny Leyland built, 'rear entry', double decker, in Cheapside, facing the 'wrong way' by today's rules. In the background is the Flag Market with the Sessions House beyond. On the right is the blackened remnant of Scott's town hall, soon to be demolished in 1960. Bus No. 122 was bought in 1951 and saw service long enough to run in the newer colours of blue and royal ivory (cream), which the horse trams had sported, before they were withdrawn in 1972.

Fishergate, corner of Butler Street 1955. Bought at the same time as No. 122, this vehicle did not survive to be painted blue and cream. From January 1948 the Corporation ran some services jointly with the Ribble Motor Services, one being the P1. This was a combination of the Frenchwood and Ashton routes, running from Frenchwood to Lea through the town centre. Ribble provided one bus out of seven to run a Monday to Saturday service. Originally the buses had three narrow bands of cream and maroon but the bodywork of the 1951 buses, known as 'Farington', only allowed one strip.

Miller Arcade: Jacson Street, c. 1965. The first service to run to Gamull Lane began in April 1937 and ran a route similar to the Holme Slack but down St. Thomas's Road, onto Deepdale Road, instead of St. George's Road. This type of bus, bought in 1958 and running until 1971, was the first 8ft wide vehicle. Its 30ft length caused problems on certain routes with narrow streets and sharp corners such as Lane Ends, Holme Slack and Moor Nook.

Fishwick bus station, Fox Street, c. 1955. Another ordinary corner of Preston now gone, where the buses of J. Fishwick and Co. of Leyland terminated their Leyland to Preston route. This bus is about to make the return journey, turning left into Fox Street and left again into Fleet Street before proceeding up Corporation Street. Nowadays Fishwicks use the Central Bus Station and the Fox Street/Fleet Street corner is blocked off. The bus station above is now a car park, made even larger by the demolition of the post office building behind.

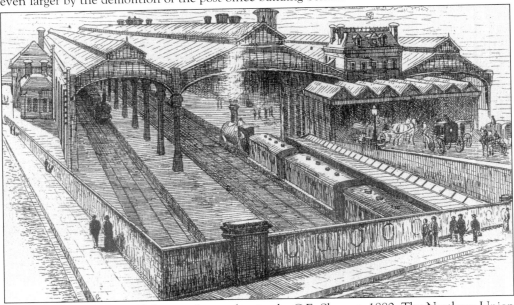

Preston Railway Station, Fishergate from a drawing by C.E. Shaw, c. 1880. The Northern Union Railway reached Preston in 1838 and was joined by other companies running neighbouring routes which resulted in Preston, having five stations for a time. Demand outpaced the central station's development and regular widening and additional tracks made Fishergate tunnel a bottleneck, especially as some trains ended at Preston and had to change engines. The first footbridge was built in 1855, before which passengers had to cross the tracks.

The *Duchess of Kent* enters Preston station, platform 7 on 3 May 1958. Confusion and frustration was common in the station's early days. Preston was a meal stop station but passengers had little time to benefit from it. During the 1862 Guild about 500,000 people came and went through here. In 1866 part of the roof fell in. When agreements were finally made between disputing railway companies, Fishergate bridge was built in 1873 and a new platform and glass roof were aded in 1879. Extensions in 1880, 1903 and 1913 gave the station its basic modern appearance. Both Queen Victoria and Tsar Nicholas II, on different occasions, dined at the station dining room.

LMS No. 42290 leaving East Lancs platform, May 1961. This view was taken from Vicars Bridge, due south of Fishergate and named presumably, because the Parish Church vicarage was nearby. Also nearby, behind the camera, was the Park Hotel, run for the convenience of rail travellers. To the right are the Butler Street goods shed and yard, which is now occupied by the Fishergate Centre and car park. Until 1921, when they amalgamated, the East Lancs and the Lancs and Yorks Railways owned two different parts of the station, each with its own stationmaster.

Locomotive No. 4421 approaching Preston from the north, 1 July 1939.. Of the apparent multitude of tracks running through this area some ran to the left to the engine shed, others to the right to Longridge (now redundant). The next split at Maudland, west to Blackpool and the Fylde and north to Scotland. This train is running along the latter, with Maudland engine shed to the right. Running along the background is Pedder Street, with its bridge and with St Walburge's (Talbot) school on the far left.

Locomotive No. 44982 entering Preston, 31 July 1965. This train has just passed St Walburge's church with its massive spire, a landmark for rail travellers. It is passing over Maudland Junction where over a dozen lines peeled off from or crossed each other into branch lines or sidings. The main control for all of this was the large signal box, Preston No. 5, which had 114 working levers to work a dozen or more signals in their combinations and the many points directing trains along the right lines. On electrification in 1973 the signal boxes became redundant.

Eight
Along the River

The Ribble from Redscar, 1855. The river rises at Ribblehead, north of Horton in Ribblesdale, from the confluence of two becks, the Cam and the Gayle, in an area where there are many springs. By the time it has reached this point the Ribble has flowed over sixty miles. In this view from Redscar the River sweeps round the bend from left to right. On the left is Nab Wood and on the right, Red Scar Wood with Seed Park in the distance.

Ribble Bridge at Walton-le-Dale drawn by C.E. Shaw, *c.* 1880. The Civil War Battle of Preston had its second phase on the 17 August 1648 around old Walton Bridge which was crooked and narrow. The road to it veered from the present bridge, opposite the Bridge Inn. The path in the drawing could be a relic of it. Unit 1755 this was the only river bridge in Preston and was built in 1625 with five arches. It was replaced by the present bridge which was widened in 1936. Calvert's cotton mill is on the right.

The Bridge at Walton-le-Dale, *c.* 1906. On the right are the beginnings of Frenchwood Boulevard. Calvert's cotton mill on the 'Flats' is on the right. To the left, opposite the factory, is a group of streets , including south and north Ribble Streets, which were flooded around this time. The white building is the Bridge Inn, owned by Samuel Garrett, newly arrived from Blackpool. He brewed his own ale and had stabling for nine horses. Diagonally out of shot, across the bridge, was Garrett's main rival, the Shawe's Arms.

Tram Bridge from Penwortham, 1906. The story of this bridge is well known, but what is remarkable is that it not only outlived its original industrial purpose, but also survived collision, flood and dilapidation to be rebuilt and kept in use. On the horizon, on the left, are the roofs of houses on East Cliff. In the centre is Avenham Incline, up which coal trucks were hauled until 1859. Avenham Tower, now slightly changed, and the houses on Bank Parade, loom through the trees. The paths on the right lead to Frenchwood.

The Ribble looking west from Avenham Walk, c. 1855. This view, no longer possible because of trees planted in 1863, shows the two railway bridges. The nearest, the East Lancs, was built in 1838 for £76,000 and has three one hundred foot spans and incorporates a walkway. To the left are five of the fifty-two arches which extended south. These were filled during 1884-6 because of flood damage. Beyond is the Northern Union, built in 1838 for £70,000, much changed over the years through rebuilding. By 1840 these bridges were said to be carrying the heaviest rail traffic in Britain.

Avenham Valley from the vicarage garden, *c.* 1855. Lacking the vegetation and trees of modern times, this is the view from the garden of the vicar of Preston. On the left is Avenham Tower on Avenham Brow and near to it is a smoking chimney of the steam engine that hauled coal trucks from Tram Bridge, seemingly striding across the river. Among the orchards can be seen Jackson's Cottage and animals grazing peacefully on South Meadow fields, soon to be Avenham Park, adopted and set out between 1862-5. This view would now be obscured by trees.

Pleasure boating on the Ribble, *c.* 1905. On a tranquil and sunny Edwardian afternoon in spring, people mess about in boats provided by John Crook, who lived on Ribbleside. Branches from a lime tree on the Avenham Park side frame a view of the river at equilibrium, between low and high tide. The river may look peaceful here but accidents were not uncommon. The lack of a weir being one reason. Boating finished on the river before the war.

A garden party at West Cliff, summer 1905. 'Do you recognise anybody?' is the message on this postcard, sent to an employee at the Midland Railway offices in Victoria Buildings, Fishergate. It seems to be a works 'do' or a sports function organised by Preston Cricket Club on whose ground it is taking place. Preston had the largest club ground in Britain at the time. Although this is fancy dress, the field placings seem serious enough with policemen at mid-wicket and cover, and Little Bo-Peep at square leg. In the background is the Park Hotel, by this time twenty five years old, which was becoming more accepted by Prestonians. When it was first built in 1882 its Ruabon red brick had been thought too bright. Alongside runs the main railway line with the Preston side of the bridge over the Ribble on the right. The hotel, closed in 1950, is now the property of Lancashire County Council. It stands on ground once occupied by a house known as The Cliff. 'Cliff' is a dominant name in this area, the original fields and parcels of land having that word combined with 'Square', 'Narrow', 'Long' and 'Round'. Neighbouring areas are now East Cliff and West Cliff, with streets named Cliff and North Cliff. The trees on the embankment are twice as tall today, but not tall enough to hide the glass box of an office block built next to the hotel in the 1950s.

Flood in Broadgate, 1926. The last flood was in the mid 1970s when the Holme and Middleforth, across the River from Broadgate, largely disappeared under water. Modern banking and retaining walls have prevented repetitions. Until the first bridge was built across the Ribble from Penwortham in 1755 (rebuilt in 1759), access to Broadgate was only possible by ferry or across the ford on Penwortham Holme. 'Holm' and 'gate' are Norse words for 'island' and 'street'.

Floodwater in Winckley Road, Broadgate, 1912. Worried residents look out over barricaded doorways. Broadgate, seen here in the distance, became an important road when the first bridge was erected. Its present houses, built in the late Victorian period, were mainly occupied by wealthy people of independent means. At No. 39 lived Mr A.J. Berry, Director of Preston Education, who organised the much loved and unsurpassed 1922 Children's Guild Pageant.

The Ribble from Church Brow, Penwortham, *c.* 1900. This view of the river as it sweeps out of Avenham Valley, was taken from the path leading up to St Mary's church. In the foreground is Penwortham Holme, once an island, where William 'Buffalo Bill' Cody brought his Wild West show in 1904. Beyond this is the row of trees on Broadgate and Penwortham Old Bridge. Thought now to be a fine example of its period, it was regarded by Anthony Hewitson in 1880 as 'narrow, high backed and inconvenient'. Beyond it is the plate girdered West Lancs Railway Bridge which was demolished after the closure of the Penwortham to Fishergate Hill section in 1900. This view would now be obscured by trees.

Preston and the Ribble from Penwortham, *c.* 1830. The Industrial Revolution has moved unto a second stage, factory chimneys outnumber the windmills, though the residents of Friargate may still have worked in fields North of Fylde Street to bring in the harvest while still employed in cotton at home or in the factory. The largest windmills were at Fylde Street (where Shutt's mill used to be), near the corner of Church Street and Deepdale Road, and Moor Lane whose main structure still exists.

Preston from Power Station Road, *c.* 1950. The Ribble is in the bottom corner, showing a small quay which was about 400yd west of Fishergate. In the foreground are the Dock Offices and various storage areas and bonded warehouses. A number of goods trains, with heavy freight and petrol tankers can be seen, the responsibility of the Ribble Branch or Dock Railway. On the right (centre) are the premises of English Electric and Dick, Kerr Ltd, opposite each other on Strand Road. To the left are a group of mills and their chimneys, situated across Water Lane, namely, from left to right: Ashton Mill (near Tulketh Brow), Shelley Road Mill, Progress (Shelley Road), Eldon Street, with Queen's Mill, Oxheys, Greenbank and Moor Hey in the distance. St Mark's church stands squarely among it all on its ridge, 90ft above sea level with Wellington Street and West View Terrace stretching to the left. In the distance. Fairsnape and Parlick fells can be seen - so rain was due!

Nine
A Walk in the Park

View from below Avenham Walk, *c.* 1935. This is one stage down from the level of Avenham Walk itself. Two Sebastopol cannons once stood here'. Across the Ribble is an area known as the Mains with Carr Wood and Dewhurst Clough in the distance. Down the next flight of steps are Riverside and Tram Bridge and the path to Frenchwood runs to the left.

South east corner of Avenham Park, *c*. 1910. All paths from here lead to Frenchwood and the railings presumably mark the boundary of the park. The path to the left leads to Selbourne Street and Frenchwood Knoll, while the central one runs over what was once known as Little Avenham Brow. The trees are said to be the relics of ancient woodland and after a period of neglect this secluded area has now been reclaimed and the steps have been built up further. Notice the children pose for the photograph in a rather oddly spaced out way for the photographer.

Forty Steps, Little Avenham Brow, *c.* 1905. Nearly 100yd further to the right are these steps, shown as one of a series of images of Avenham in snow. This is now part of the reclaimed area where widflowers thrive; Lords-and-Ladies, Wood Anenomes and the Bearded Couch, Corn Marigolds, Corn Cockles and Corn Poppies. Wild birds visit and the Chiffchaff, the Blackcap and the Willow Warbler are among the visitors. The steps, now rebuilt, number more than forty.

Avenham Tower from Avenham Walk, c. 1903. The Italian-style tower was built in 1847 by the Threlfall family and is a familiar landmark, though it looks different now, having lost its balcony and overhanging roof. For the first twelve years of its existence it was faced, across the Walk, by the working stationary steam engine that noisily pulled up coal trucks from Tram Bridge, belching smoke from its chimney. For a further ten years the derelict engine-house remained until the site was occupied by the Belvedere.

The Bandstand, Avenham Park from a drawing by Edwin Beattie, 1903. From 1891, Edwin Beattie (1845-1917) recorded Preston's buildings and streets, especially those which were ancient or near to demolition. During the 1890s he was busiest, working independently and for the *Preston Guardian*, who let him go in March 1899 when they were able to reproduce photographs with the new photogravure method. This postcard picture may be an example of turning his hand to something else. It is a clever record of detail. The Park Hotel and East Cliff houses are featured, and through the bandstand, the cottage by the East Lancs Railway bridge can be seen.

The Duck Pond, Avenham Park, 1902. The Corporation bought land in Avenham Valley as early as 1844 and by 1852 held all area occupied by the Park. between 1862 and 1867, using unemployed men during the cotton famine, the Valley was transformed and in the north west corner, Edward Milner, the landscape architect laid out the Duck Pond, described by Hewitson as a 'lakelet, with a rustic, rock-formed cascade in the rear'. In 1936, using 130 tons of Milnthorpe stone, it was redesigned into the Japanese Rock Garden.

View from the Derby Terrace, Miller Park, 1909. Once described by the Edwardian writer, A.J. Berry, as a 'real fairyland', the park is still remarkable, especially in summer. The land was given to the town by Thomas Miller, alderman and cotton master, who died in 1865 before the Park was finished. This and Avenham Park were places of relaxation for many of the local factory operatives.

Miller Park from behind the Derby statue, photographed by D.G. Cranston in 1952. This view was originally called 'Lord Derby's View' and shows the park with the river and railway bridge in the distance, the fountain and ornamental pond and, to the left, the old aviary. The statue is of Edward Stanley, 14th Earl of Derby, MP for Preston and eventual Prime Minister who donated £500 to aid poor families during the cotton famine. The statue cost £2,000, with £349 of it coming from work people's penny subscriptions.

Miller Park on Easter Monday 1905. The fountain was always a focal point. It was installed in 1868 and promised jets of water rising to 60ft. The jets are set in the shell which is supported by the Four Elements - Earth, Air, Fire and Water, represented by sculpted female figures. It was restored for the 1992 Guild.

The Garden Entrance to the Park Hotel, c. 1920. This is the view which would have greeted visitors arriving on foot from Miller Park through the stone gateway and past the flowerbeds. On the right is the ornate portico leading to a large vestibule and reception area. This Western aspect is still possible today, though both levels are car parks and the park entrance is dwarfed by a 1950s office block, mercifully out of view at this angle. The interior of the 'Hotel' building is being gradually restored by Lancashire County Council.

Preston, Park Hotel.

The Park Hotel and Sun Dial Gardens, c. 1905. This view shows a scene now hidden by a screen of mature trees, so the Hotel, once a favourite stopping place for music hall artists, sports stars and politicians, can no longer be seen from this angle. The Sun Dial Gardens are a riot of colour in summer and were described by Hewitson, a little after 1880, when they were set out, as 'exquisite flowerbeds'. To the left are the trees and bushes round the Grotto.

The Grotto, Miller Park, c. 1905. The Grotto, which is situated in partial obscurity in the north west corner, is a lasting testament to Edward Milner who designed Miller Park. This shows where the path runs under robust arrangements of large, rough boulders in a seemingly natural setting. On the left are three steps, and to the girl's right is a cascade that flows over different shelves of rocks into a green pool, in turn flowing under the path into another pool near the Sun Dial Gardens.

The Grotto, c. 1905. Both this and the previous photograph were issued by Heywoods of Fishergate and show different entrances. The Grotto can be entered by a third route, from West Cliff, and then to a level above the girls' heads, before turning down to the three steps at the back. The whole construction is full of contrasts; shades of light and dark, daylight and shadows with intriguing levels of bridges and steps. Edward Milner, who set out Preston's Victorian parks, worked under Sir Joseph Paxton (1803-65) at Chatsworth.

Frenchwood Bowling Club, George Street, Frenchwood, *c.* 1950. The houses, just visible, top right, are on Larkhill Street and the trees to the left, planted over a century earlier by the Horrocks family, then of Lark Hill House, provide a picturesque setting.

Acknowledgements

Without the help of certain people this book would not have been possible. I would like to thank Brenda and Norman Worthington very much for lending me pictures of street scenes from their collection. I would like to thank Alice Lakeland for the gift of some views round St Augustine's. I am grateful to Andrew Walmsley for his help in locating the Victorian line drawings from Peter Whittle's *History of Preston*. Other books I have consulted while compiling this book include books by Anthony Hewitson (with some care!), Margaret Burscough and Carole Knight's history of Fulwood, and works by Gordon Biddle, Stuart Taylor, T.C. Dickinson and Mike Rhodes.

I also received all kinds of other help from many people: Lillian Counsell gave me a tour of the ground floor of the Park Hotel building, where she advises on its redecoration, Eddie Curry of Preston Borough's Leisure Services passed me information about Milner's connection with the town and Phil Garlington, the photographer, who allowed me to use pictures.

For kind permission to reproduce photographs from their handbooks I would like to thank Preston Borough Council. I have also used a few excellent images from a collection of prizewinning photographs from the 1952 Guild Photography Competition. Despite extensive efforts I was unable to make contact with any of the amateur photographers concerned and have decided to use their photographs in the book and hope that, by bringing them into the open again in this way, those concerned will be pleased rather than annoyed. Each of these photographs is fully acknowledged in the book.

I wish to thank Michelle Coulton and Michelle Cox, pupils at All Hallows Catholic School where I teach, who word processed two thirds of the text for me. I am very grateful to them both and wish them well for the future.

I would like to thank David Buxton of Tempus Publishing for the chance of writing this second selection. I appreciate his friendly advice and encouragement. I have also been encouraged by friends and family, especially my daughters, Ruth and Beth, and my wife, Nina. I would like to thank them also for their patience and support, especially when the going was tough. As ever, I tried carefully to avoid putting Nina in the state of Mrs Gradgrind of *Hard Times* who was often '...stunned by some weighty piece of fact tumbling on her'!